Careers by Design

A Headhunter's Secrets
for Success and Survival
in Graphic Design

by Roz Goldfarb

Introductions by Miho
and Ramone Munoz

ALLWORTH PRESS, NEW YORK
Copublished with the American Council for the Arts

Careers by Design

#28195589

Published by Allworth Press,
an imprint of Allworth Communications, Inc.
10 East 23rd Street, New York, NY 10010.

Distributor to the trade in the United States:
Consortium Book Sales & Distribution, Inc.
1045 Westgate Drive, Saint Paul, MN 55114–1065.

Distributor to the art material trade:
Arthur Schwartz & Co.
234 Meads Mountain Road, Woodstock, NY 12498.

Distributor to the trade in Canada:
Raincoast Books Distribution Limited
112 East 3rd Avenue, Vancouver, B.C. V5T 1C8

Book and cover design by
Michael Bierut, Pentagram Design, New York, NY.

ISBN: 1-880559-05-6

Library of Congress Catalog Card Number: 92-75527

Contents

Contents

Contents

Contents

Introduction

Pythagoras (c582-c507 BC) believed that all things were in numbers and that numbers guide people to limits and to the unlimited (imagination). These important contributions were made to medicine, music, and astronomy. The limits in the Arctic Circle were guided by two concepts: adaptation and constant change, based on strong tradition through experience. So it is with graphic designers who adapt and change globally but who develop from a strong ethos of conceptual thinking. This book is a guide, a map, a dictionary and a reference book for beginners and for those seeking change to better themselves — it's about time too!

Miho
Chairman, Graphic Design Department
Art Center College of Design

Introduction

At a recent graduation at Art Center, the graduation speaker, Phil Jueano, Chairman of the Board of Daiely Associates, gave the following simple advice to the 125 eager graduating students who were about to move into nine different design-related fields. He told the group before him that they had a better chance of achieving success in their fields if they were to 1) work hard, 2) do a good job and 3) never give up.

Simple Advice Is Not Always Simple

Simple yet profound advice to be sure. So is that found in this extraordinary new book by Roz Goldfarb which helps the young student as well as the seasoned professional to establish a rock solid foundation for the good advice expressed by Phil Jueano. The difference lies in that where Mr. Jueano's advice may seem a bit vague or general in nature, Mrs. Goldfarb's book is anything but vague or general. In fact, this remarkable guide may well be the most comprehensive book published to date on exactly who graphic designers are and what they do. This book fills the gap which currently exists in all design fields regarding the student's preparation for the real world. Having taught college design courses over the last twelve years, I can honestly say that I have not yet seen anything approaching the comprehensive nature of this guide that I could recommend to students.

Roz Goldfarb's use of highly insightful analogies, metaphors and countless recollections from actual experience as the owner of one of America's leading placement agencies in the field of design, makes this guide a pleasure to digest and extremely memorable for all of its detail.

The Job Market – Yesterday, Today and Tomorrow

In dealing with the harsh realities of the current professional job market, I continue to be amazed at the perception of young designers about their employers and/or clients. Many students and even some professionals seem to think that they are hired because their clients like them and want to help them make beautiful, award-winning design. A sort of loving partnership towards similar aesthetic goals. This, of course, is rarely the case. By and large designers and design firms are hired to help promote products and services resulting in profits for the client and, hopefully, a prolonged and profitable relationship with the designer or the design firm. Students and young designers also fail to consider their own true value to the design firms they work for or the clients they serve. If this guide does anything, it surely amplifies this crucial concept; designers are valuable, very valuable, and the world of commerce needs us as much as we need them, not only for the perpetuation of sound economics but also for the betterment, through the design/arts, of society in general. The clearer these ideas form themselves in the minds of designers, the more professionally they will handle their own careers.

The Good Old Days Are Always Today

I have often heard designers, some fresh out of school, and others who have been in the field a while, complain about how the economy has hurt business, how much better things were at some other time and that better days will, hopefully, be around the corner. This, in my opinion, is simply an excuse for creative people who are not very good at assessing their own value and presenting that value to the marketplace. The designers I respect are always busy, regardless of the economic climate, and those complaining about hard times will undoubtedly complain in any business climate. Again, it boils down to knowing what you are doing and making sure that others know it too. A lean business economy may actually weed out mediocre designers and this, in the final analysis, is probably a good thing — the survival of the fittest.

Physician Heal Thyself

The graphic design profession faces the great challenge of a general public and a business community which, in most cases, is totally uneducated regarding design and qualitative issues related to design. In essence, designers face the day-to-day problem of trying to sell services whose value may be quite unclear to clients. In this respect, I feel that this book can greatly serve young as well as established designers in defining the vast nature of this business, not only for our own clarification as designers, but also for the education of clients. I am sure that all designers can identify with the painstaking process of trying to write their own capabilities brochure. I remember going through the exercise for my own design office, trying to piece together definitions from dozens of books on design. Writing and rewriting, shelving the whole process in frustration, starting up again when it becomes apparent that the identity program we were losing was our own and that it was costing us a lot of business. Any designer or design firm contemplating the development of their own capability brochure will find that Roz has painstakingly described the many services we provide clients in such a concise manner that I get excited about the profession just reading them. I guarantee that you'll find them to be a priceless guide in explaining who we are as designers and what we do.

The Ever Present Future

It is often the case that anyone attempting to write about computers is either writing about science fiction or archaeology. Anyone involved in this form of creative Andromeda strain knows that the subject defies definition because it simply won't sit still. Having worked closely with our computer development, I know that everything that Roz has stated is true and reflects accurately all aspects of what the student, young designer or design firm should know about this dynamic medium. What impressed me the most is the emphasis

Roz and her associates place on the computer's capacity to seduce and then abandon anyone who thinks that this technology can think and design for the designer. Roz emphasizes time as well as the overriding importance of good conceptual thinking supported by a broad liberal arts and science background. Roz clarifies what we all know in design education — that the computer is simply a tool which can empower the educated designer or produce catastrophes in the hands of those who "know not what they do."

So You've Become a Designer – So What?

Design schools are currently unleashing thousands of students into the professional arena each year. Sadly, many of these students will be ill-equipped to present themselves to the design community with their best foot forward. In fact, many will end up getting in their own way.

I'll never forget visiting a friend of mine, a creative directive director at a large Madison Avenue advertising agency, one late afternoon while on vacation in Manhattan. I got into the elevator destined for the ionosphere when three young men entered all carrying portfolios. Two of the men who seemed to be friends were rather casually dressed and carried rather shabby looking portfolios. The third man wore a business suit and tie, sported a new portfolio and had an air of confidence about him. As the elevator rose into the clouds, the two friends talked about their chances of landing a design job which was apparently open at my friend's agency. The two friends could not help but notice the well-dressed fellow with the new portfolio and shyly asked if he was interviewing for the same position. After answering with a highly confident "yes," the two friends asked where he had received his degree. On hearing his answer, one of the two other fellows said, and I quote: "I guess this counts us out." They pushed the elevator button and got out before reaching the agency. I'll never forget this incident, and, as a teacher, it stands as an ever-present reminder of the responsibility which educational institutions have — not simply to give students a piece of paper which says "College Degree" but to give them something vastly more important. Students need a clear understanding of themselves as dynamic individuals empowered with the tools, not simply to survive in this or any business climate, but to excel to the absolute fullest extent of their abilities. After all, even the best student can work hard, do good work and be tenacious and still not be noticed. I feel that this superb guidebook can truly help make the difference for students and professionals alike between simply finding a job or establishing a career. Having read this invaluable book, my only disappointment is that, at the time of the writing of this introduction, the book is not yet published and available to my students. I assure you, for what it's worth, the moment it becomes available, it will also become mandatory reading for all undergraduate and post-graduate graphic design students at the Art Center College of Design. Roz, I salute you, not only for having provided students and professionals alike with this invaluable tool for enhancing our understanding of ourselves and helping us to supercharge our careers, but also for having made a great educational contribution to the very nature of understanding design and its advancement in the world business community. THANK YOU seems hardly appropriate for such a great effort.

Ramone C. Munoz
Chairman of Foundation Studies and
Coordinator of Graduate Research in Graphic Design
Art Center College of Design

Foreword

Life is a series of choices. To my mind, choice is perhaps the key player in the game of life. Being able to make informed choices means having freedom. It means having the freedom to choose and direct the course of your future, the freedom to change directions and the freedom to feel in control of your actions. This kind of freedom does not come easily. It requires a commitment to work, research, and to yourself. Truthfully, I also think it requires a certain amount of luck. But if you are worldly and aware it is amazing how "luck" can find you. There are people who make their opportunities happen and those who wouldn't recognize an opportunity if it stared them in the face.

The information required to function with "freedom of choice" falls into three categories.

- You must have the proper education — the exposure to the concepts and tools necessary for your personal development.

- You must have the ambition and commitment to want to do your personal best.

- You must be knowledgeable and informed about your chosen career and the world at large.

After a 20 year-career in Design Placement and Design Education, I'm continually amazed to learn what little information exists on the hard-core issues of the design business. The concept of design as a business is clearly the focus of this book for that is what it is — a business. To achieve this end, you will require an understanding of the structure of business and how the various components of design interrelate to each other and to graphic design as a whole. It's the ability to see the forest and be able to discern different species of trees.

Life Choices

This is the kind of information that would enable students, professionals, career counselors, and educators to make important life choices.

For some people, these initial choices, made early in life, often determine unalterable courses. I often refer to my "Smorgasbord Theory of Choice" when lecturing to students. This theorem goes like this: Pretend you're at a wedding reception and you are presented with a very long smorgasbord. You are only allowed one plate. You therefore get in line, take a plate, and start to fill it with wonderful, delicious food. The only problem is, as your plate fills up, you realize you haven't reached the end of the table. As you approach the end you see the selection is better and you'd prefer that food — but, you have no more room on your dish! Had you only known! You now realize it would have been wiser to have scanned the length of the table before getting in line. Although life does not allow us to scan the length of our table before getting in line, there are some things we can control through knowledge. Choosing a career or making a career change at least affords us an educated guess and with the information in this book, a much broader concept of what awaits.

Too often I have interviewed people well on in their careers who have held a vague notion of which paths their careers might travel. And as for the young, they were only propelled by an intuitive recognition that they were "talented" and were lacking any real sense of field they wished to enter. Artistic talent usually surfaces very early in life. Most creative people first recognize that part of their personality when they are young children and in later years acknowledge a need to find a practical application of their abilities. When that interest turns to design it is a rare person who has an informed, realistic picture of what graphic design is about, how it relates

to advertising, and where in the scheme of things he fits in —
for most people it's totally unclear.

**The Need For
Career
Information**

Logically, if career information is needed, high school
students and their parents will attempt to seek out help from
guidance counselors and art teachers. Unfortunately, these
individuals rarely have the necessary information either.
Their own education and life experience has not given them
enough exposure. While I was the Director of the Pratt
Phoenix School of Design (a division of Pratt Institute) in the
late 1970's, I ran a continuing education program for the
New York City Board of Education's high school teachers.
These short seminars were designed to offer an overview of
the different areas of design, the opportunities available, the
basic job descriptions and what people working in these fields
earned. It proved to be an eye-opener, for many of these
teachers were either guidance counselors or art teachers who
never had contact with such direct and pragmatic information. It should be noted that, in most cases, accurate data is
available from the admissions offices of art colleges that
specialize in professional programs. There are several professional design colleges in this county (see Index), but it should
be indicated that most of them have a specific educational
point of view and specialization within their curricula. (See
Chapter 14.)

**How My Opinions
Were Formed**

It is important for the readers of this book to know how
and why my opinions were formed. After nearly 10 years as
an administrator and educator at Pratt Institute, I joined an
executive recruitment firm specializing in placing designers
and art directors in jobs within the design and advertising
fields. While at Pratt I became aware of the urgent need for
proper career information — something I never had. At that
time my efforts were directed toward developing courses,
workshops and seminars for high school and college level

students and teachers. As a recruiter, and now as president of my own firm, Roz Goldfarb Associates, I'm subjected daily to the vicissitudes of hiring criteria and firing practices, to the demands employers place on their staff, and to the frustrations people experience in the workplace on both sides of the fence. I have been given the unique opportunity of observing careers in the making as well as observing careers that flounder. And I see these occurrences from a very special vantage

A Special Vantage Point

point, for we are the consultants whose very existence depends on our ability to keep a confidence. Our clients range from the design gurus, — the movers and shakers whose fame precedes them — to small entrepreneurs, and all others who recognize that their business' success depends on the quality of their creative personnel. Both our clients (those who pay our fees to find them the "perfect person") and our candidates (those who wish another career opportunity and position) confide their motivations to us, knowing that information is necessary for us to function accurately and knowing it will be kept in confidence. The vast number of negotiations of profound, fundamental decision making choices we experience in the daily drama of our office by far outstrip the designer or art director who has probably (and hopefully) changed jobs less than 10 times in a lifetime. I will draw upon these experiences in this book through case histories or anecdotes, but of course names will never be divulged.

In entering into any overview of design, clear professional distinctions must be made between design and advertising; the types of jobs that will form careers which are realistic and possible; what one can expect to earn in these positions; and what kind of a lifestyle that may dictate. With proper information, and more than a little good luck, an informed decision for a life choice or career change is possible. I hope we can provide a guide to entering a fascinating world and to some of its opportunities. As I've mentioned, you can't make a decision if you don't know what the choices are. Too often we're asked to do just that! Often at Pratt, I would encounter an irate parent, who strongly believed the investment of time and money into an art education was impractical and wasteful. I'll never forget the student applying to Pratt Institute who tearfully told me why he couldn't accept our offer of admission and partial scholarship. His father, a teacher, would have gladly paid for his education if he were to become an accountant or the like, but would never contribute his hard-earned money to further a design education. Nor would the father allow me the opportunity to explain that one could earn a respectful and sometimes highly compensated income in design and that his son could achieve the personal gratification necessary for a complete life.

The graphic designer holds a unique position in our expanding world of communications. While the design business has grown and matured substantially in the United States,

The Graphic Designer's Unique Position

there is still little public recognition of its impact on our everyday existence. Simply put, everything we wear, touch, read, ride in and live in has been created by a designer. Our newspapers, magazines, and books, our household appliances and automobiles, the packages that cover every object imaginable and entice us to buy, the graphic images, logotypes, and signs in stores and restaurants, their identity, menus and even sometimes their names, the amusement parks we take our children to, the famous cartoon characters we become attached to, the licensed products we buy with their logos or images; the shapes of cosmetic jars, bottles, compacts, lipsticks and their packaging; the gift wrap and cards for presents, the incalculable numbers of brochures, annual reports and corporate literature — all have been developed or designed by graphic and industrial designers. The list is endless.

Design Is a Business

And most important, design is a business. It is not enough to want to create something that is beautiful. Design awards and professional recognition are tremendous incentives. Sometimes a design will even enter the collection of a famous museum. But design must also reflect a responsiveness to market factors, and designers must be knowledgeable about sociological and economic trends. Today we all are well aware of being members of a global economic community. The design community, as part of the business community, has played an integral part in these developments. Many firms have an international reach through either branch offices or a multinational client base. Therefore anyone entering these fields must recognize the need for an increased level of participation in the essential core of the business in order to make the important decisions resulting in career and life choices.

This book's goal is to identify the distinctions between various areas of specialization, to analyze the talent and personality most apt to thrive, to point to the newer, developing areas where increased opportunity may lie and to give an approximation of the salary levels currently prevalent in these fields. Generalizations are always dangerous, but this book will try to discern the characteristics of major market segments as well as look to the future.

In defining graphic design, I have included a discussion of industrial design only in its relationship to graphic design. I have eliminated the associated fields of photography and illustration. Both are formidable creative areas practiced by many designers. However while graphic designers may utilize photography and illustration in their own work, or art direct photographers and illustrators, the converse is rarely true. Photographers and illustrators are rarely graphic designers. And the exceptional people who do it all are legendary. This book is geared to the student, the young professional, the established professional seeking change and to the art educator. It is designed to inform in a concise manner, for quick reference, and from a point of view acquired through years of dealing with everyday, real world life experiences.

I want to express my personal thanks and gratitude to Rita Armstrong and Tom Weisz. Tom Weisz has always been the enthusiastic visionary pushing me and everyone else, ready or not, into the future. Rita Armstrong, as an Roz Goldfarb Associate and the youngest member of my firm, has been the mature counselor that everyone needs. She has provided the on-line information for job placement of computer designers from her day-to-day experiences. I'm very lucky.

Ultimately we all are the sum of our experiences. My professional life has continuously been enriched through the fellowship of many very talented and sometimes brilliant people of vastly divergent viewpoints. This diversity in itself has educated me for I have always been fascinated by their life experiences and business philosophies. Having an open mind, listening intently, evaluating, accepting and rejecting viewpoints has allowed me to formulate many of my own opinions. It would be negligent for me not to mention a few of these individuals. The following list are those who are perhaps most apparent but certainly there are many more. In New York: Ron Peterson of Peterson Blyth (who not only gave me good counsel, but a sofa for my office!); Clive Chajet, the CEO of Lippincott & Margulies; all the folks — past and present — at Siegel & Gale, Alan Siegel, Don Ervin, Ken Cooke; Steff Geisbuhler, a Principal of Chermayeff & Geismar; Anthony Russell; Michael Peters in London; in Los Angeles Saul Bass and Herb Yager; Gerry Rosentzweig; the educators at Art Center College of Design; Michael Cronan, Primo Angeli and John Crane in San Francisco; Henry Steiner

Thanks!

in Hong Kong; the thousands of people all over the country who I have interviewed and generously shared their perceptions, dreams and frustrations; and not least the staff and faculty of Pratt Institute in Brooklyn who, as a member of their team, enabled me to begin this journey into design.

And thanks are due to the associates of Roz Goldfarb Associates. They are Marion Thunberg, Rita Armstrong, Penny Burrow, Connie Kail Wolf and Elaine Oxenberg. We are, in addition to an integrated business unit, much like an extended family. I am surrounded by unique people and I'm in matchless company.

Finally there's my family, who, at the end of the day, are the most important focus of my world. My mother, now 87, owned a dress factory in New York's very tough garment center before anyone ever thought of women's liberation. She set us all quite an example. My husband Ben, my partner and best friend; our three daughters Meryl, Leslie, and Jessica who are making their own life's choices; and our grandson, Matthew, our next generation — all are precious beyond description.

I'll close with a toast to all those not mentioned, who have given me the opportunity to learn and those who, no doubt, will be part of my future. All have allowed me to experience the fruit my life's choices.

Roz Goldfarb

What Is Graphic Design?

1

How many people can indeed give a reasonable definition of graphic design? It's not a profession that has a clear identity in the mind of the general public. Design is a much used word, and can mean many things. Often when people refer to designers they may have a generalized notion of fashion design or engineering design, as well as automotive, product and architectural design, and perhaps industrial design. But usually graphic design is grouped with that ubiquitous term "advertising." Advertising is, after all, well-known. We have seen it in film and fiction. It's all-pervasive in our society but it's not design. Tell someone at a party you're a graphic designer and you'll probably find they will consider you part of the advertising world or confuse your job with graphic reproduction and the printing industries. Or, worse, somebody may say, "Oh, I understand, you're a commercial artist," which is a totally archaic term. The public believes it knows what architecture, interior design or advertising is about, but the identifier graphic design can be a mystery. It's interesting to note the amount of confusion among educators and other professionals as well. Few can identify the difference between an industrial designer, environmental designer, or graphic designer.

The Designer's Role in Society and Business

While Design has not traditionally been one of the glamour professions, fame may soon be awaiting the anonymous designer. With the advent of the 1990's, Design has become a hot media topic. Business publications are beginning to focus on the correlation between design and the success of product launches. The Wall Street Journal recently added a column entitled, "Form and Function," although it is mostly devoted to industrial design. In the special Business Week issue of August 23, 1990 themed "Innovation: The Global Race," the editors predicted: "Design is to the '90s what finance was to the '80s, and marketing to the '70s: It is the corporate buzz-word for the new decade."

The effect of good, functional design in the marketplace has long been recognized in other parts of the world. We all are aware of the impact of German, and Japanese design in the automotive field; Italian design in lighting, and fashion, and Scandinavian design in silver and furniture. It's a sad commentary about our society to realize that only recently is corporate America recognizing that good design can sell. Nonetheless, this recognition will shed new light on the profession of design and the role of the graphic designer.

Designers as Arbiters of Taste

However, while the graphic designer's role may not yet be readily identifiable, the designer does have an enormous impact on our society. Designers create the look and feel of our world. They are the arbiters of taste and establish as well as lead the way to how we perceive what's good, tasteful, stylish — or not, as the case may be. As pointed out in my forward, virtually everything around us is created through design. The diversity and global reach of the designer's influence is so vast it can be difficult to comprehend. Therefore it certainly must not be overlooked or undervalued. Designers create and interpret sociological trends. They create the mood and shape of our world. Designers, therefore, must be worldly in the true sense of the word. They must be aware of all things that affect change and style. Politics and finance, entertainment and literature, fine arts and history, food and music — all play important roles in our constantly transforming environment. In other words, they must observe and perhaps partake in all facets of life. No one entering this field should be content with a confining definition of creativity. Creativity is not just the action of the imagination and a particular skill; like drawing, writing or composing. You must also have the ability to analyze, assimilate and interpret the past and present structure of society in order to foretell the future.

As there is little in our daily experience that is not designed by designers, the graphic designer has an unusual opportunity to make a personal contribution to our world in this expand-

Design in Our Daily Experience

ing business environment. As a designer you can derive creative fulfillment from your efforts and still earn a reasonable, and in some cases sizable, income from those efforts. The combination of personal and economic satisfaction offers many individuals a gratifying avenue to apply their talent. Graphic designers, by and large, may sometimes complain about long hours and perhaps their pay scale, but mostly they are a committed and satisfied group because they can always see a tangible result of their work effort.

And design is a field which is expanding. It's an exciting time to be in graphic design. Design firms are growing in their complexity and size. Like advertising, design is becoming a global business. Mergers, joint ventures and international expansion have all combined to produce companies that are viable in the global arena.

While many firms have expanded through acquisition — such as buying out another design firm in another city — in the past few years many design firms have been acquired by advertising agencies. This is a newly developed recognition in the profitability of "below the line" companies as well as a desire to diversify the agency's services within the communications fields. The term "below the line" refers to companies without media placement. Agencies traditionally derive income from a percentage mark-up of media placement — meaning a mark-up on the dollars spent for their clients in buying time and space in broadcast (television and radio) or in print publications.

Clearing Up Some Confusion About Advertising and Design

Advertising differs from design in many ways. Advertising is always a visual and written solution to a marketing strategy. The message is to sell a product or service. The key word here is "sell." Never underestimate that intent. Whether it's television, print advertisements found in newspapers and magazines, direct mail or direct response ads, it is all there to send the message "buy me."

In most agencies the key players are the creative team working in conjunction with the marketing account executives (jokingly known as the "suits"). The creative team is composed of art directors and copywriters, who work in tandem. This combined team of creative and marketing talent devises the advertising strategy with and for the client. Each point of view offers another expertise to form the final direction. It is the media department who makes the necessary decisions for placement of the advertising in print and broadcast because they buy the space and time. Advertising is a huge business whose budgets dwarf those allocated to the design field. And as we all know, advertising is a powerful force in our media intensive society, saturating us with concepts like "The Pepsi Generation" or Chevrolet's "The Heartbeat of America."

It is important to note that the business of advertising (as well as design) is ultimately its creative product. It is the art directors and the copywriters who "make" advertising. It is this creative output which makes advertising and the various design areas a unique business. And these are service businesses, another special characteristic. They are dependent upon the quality of their product and dependent on business relationships who "buy into" or believe in the power of the work as an effective business practice. Some advertising can be tracked, to be made accountable. Mostly, however, it is far more intangible — really a perception of success.

In any discussion of advertising and design, it should be

noted that it is in sales promotion that the two disciplines meet. While sales promotion will be discussed at length in Chapter 6, let it suffice to say now that the brochures, marketing tools and point-of-sale products developed by the sales promotional divisions within advertising agencies need talent that can work with design values and marketing driven concepts. These promotion groups, at their best, offer designers opportunities to work on a variety of diversified assignments not always available in studio environments.

Therefore the two immediate distinctions between advertising and design are that (1) design firms, by definition, do not place media and (2) designers do not do print advertising and television campaigns. *When firms place media, they are considered, by definition, an agency.* In recruiting talent for our clients, the ability for designer to work with copy can frequently be a key ingredient in the job description. To work with copy means the designer must be able to visually interpret the copy concepts. Many graphic designers are more comfortable working strictly with graphic symbols and visual images without incorporating headline concepts or detailed copy.

Designers produce product and image-conscious sales tools for goods and services. Design like advertising can be produced on any scale or budget. Designers produce solutions for multi-national firms as well as export their expertise in image marketing all over the world. For example, companies such as Avon or Colgate produce product design and packaging design to be sold throughout the world. The designs of these products usually have to be altered for the marketing conditions of the geographical area and in some cases that may mean changing the name as well. An annual report or corporate brochure may be produced in many languages; a retail chain will need its graphic imaging subtly defined for another culture.

Design's Impact on Style

As the importance of design receives ever-increasing acknowledgment from the media, its impact can also be seen in the emergence of specialty gift shops marketing "design savvy" products as a sales tool. Design departments in museums have been highlighting the important role of graphic and industrial design for years. The Museum of Modern Art in New York, for example, has had a seminal role in design appreciation and has now mastered the art of merchandising chosen products through its store and catalogues. All of this attention bodes well for the growing prestige of the designer. It is a direct response to the proven influence design has on business profitability and an affirmation that design has created the look and feel of our world. Design determines how we perceive what's good, tasteful and stylish — or not — as the case may be. As noted earlier, corporate America is now recognizing what Europeans have known for a long time: That design is big business, and that it drives the marketing efforts for success. That good design sells. That a well-designed package can sell a product. Good product design can sell everything from cars to appliances. A well-designed retail image will move shoppers and merchandise. An excellent corporate identity program can affect the entire perception of the company, even on Wall Street.

The Business Issues of Design

So the bottom line is the bottom line! The importance of the graphic designer and graphic design as a profession is ultimately its impact on business. Therefore, although graphic design incorporates an aesthetic experience and a creative endeavor, it is its alliance to business, its ability to service clients' needs, that defines its place and status in today's economy. The art student pursuing a graphic design education must acknowledge design's role in the business community. Not to recognize this factor could only be an act of unnecessary idealism as well as a foolhardy conclusion. Without question the overriding common denominator of the most successful people in Graphic Design is their ability to maintain the highest creative standards without losing sight of their role as directors of a business.

I've often thought it a shame that fundamental business courses are not taught within the standard curriculum found in professional art colleges. Business insight is necessary to

The Need for Business Education

run your own business, to understand your client's businesses and to understand how to solve your client's problems. If you are going to design an annual report, you'd better be able to understand what the financial data in the back of the book represent. If you're going to design a corporate identity program, you should have the knowledge of how that corporation functions in the marketplace, what you need to convey in terms of its image and how that image will affect the company's internal structure as well as its external communications. In short, you need to know how the business community operates. Much of the "phase 1" strategies and planning for design solutions are currently assigned to account executives and marketing planners within design firms. In fact, most large design firms define themselves as "Marketing Communications Consultants." While these roles will be discussed in Chapter 3, I now want to emphasize the necessity for the student or design professional to appreciate how important it is not to think of utilizing your creative instincts in the naive vacuum of making things look "pretty." The role of the professional graphic designer is to identify the client's communication problems and to create solutions that are aesthetically pleasing, communicate a proper message to the public and to do so in a timely manner and on budget. Most hiring requests today emphasize the need for someone who is not only supremely talented, but someone "smart;" someone who understands the business needs of the firm and can verbally as well as visually communicate them.

Is Design for You?

The individual determined to seek a career in the creative arts often seems to recognize this goal from a relatively early age. The ability to draw is always admired in children and the encouragement often elicits the spoken ambition of becoming an "artist." Obviously it's a long road from those origins to identifying graphic design as the chosen path. The roots, however, are important. But out of those roots must evolve a designer with a love of typography, color and materials, with a desire to communicate through visual media. The designer must be a committed individual with a strong, determined desire to do good work. This book will point the paths through the maze of choices within graphic design.

The designer must also become a sophisticated person, knowledgeable and articulate about politics, business, all the arts — music, painting, history, food, and travel. After all, how can one successfully communicate to a society without being a full-fledged citizen of that society? To compound the issue, our society is now global, and therefore everything needed on a national basis is now a global issue.

These are the characteristics of a successful designer. The profession is stimulating in its vast breadth and exposure to every sector of the global business community. The individual who desires this direction must be prepared to enter this community with the knowledge and skills required to make a contribution.

Finally, is graphic design for you? Only you can say for sure, but you can expose yourself though this book and other resources to allow yourself an educated decision. If you have the motivation, go for it. Many people change careers during their adult lifetime. Many do not end up doing what they thought they would. It is always fascinating to ask individuals you admire what they thought they would become. The answers are often surprising.

The Structure of Graphic Design

2

We have just examined the essential nature of graphic design and familiarized ourselves with the role of the designer in our society. It is now time to consider the nature of the creative product how it services the marketing needs of business, and to discover the many parts which form the whole of graphic design. What may have seemed a simple classification is, in fact, an umbrella term for a sophisticated network of graphic-based communications disciplines. It is important to distinguish between these fields of endeavor for a clear understanding of the interrelationships within graphic design. A structural knowledge of the differing aspects of design is critical because although these aspects interface with each other individually, they connect and correlate with the whole. In addition they characteristically define the role of the professional. This perspective needs to be seen with some historical context as well, for with the passage of time and the refinement of the business, we shall see how these fragments of graphic design have often branched off to form areas of specialization.

Therefore, the perspective offered in this and the next chapters should help people realize their career goals as well as more completely understand the essential nature of graphic design. And what are we talking about when we say graphic design? Classically we mean:

- Brand Identity (branding) and Packaging Design

- Corporate Identity — visual identifiers, logotype and naming

- Corporate Communications and Corporate Literature — including corporate promotion and annual reports

- Editorial Design

- Environmental Design—two-and three-dimensional design of a space including exhibition design (also considered a part of Industrial Design)

- Retail Identity—similar to corporate identity, but applied to the retail sector

- Sales Promotion (can be an adjunct to advertising) Ask most people participating in these fields to name their profession and they'll probably respond, graphic design. While that response is, of course, true, many designers find their day-to-day work focused on only a small segment of this complex field.

The Rise of Specialization

In order to discuss these areas of specialization, as they relate to the whole and as individual fields of endeavor, let us use an old, but appropriate, metaphor. Consider this image: we are observing a large river with many smaller rivers and streams flowing into the main estuary. Can you visualize the great main waterway, its vitality and its bustling river traffic? We'll name this river Graphic Design. Now let us look at its tributaries. We will call them packaging, identity, and promotion, all flowing into and merging together to form Graphic Design. The river pilots of these tributaries understand how their water conditions, are interrelated with the main river body, but they know their branch best. The pilots of the main riverboats have far-reaching itineraries, traveling up and down all the branching rivers. These pilots enjoy the ever-changing vista and are quite flexible; however, they may have to familiarize themselves anew with waters not often traveled or they may consult with the local experts. The branch river specialists, however, while aware of the total terrain, find that by limiting themselves to servicing their own river they have gained an ever-increased knowledge of its waters. And whenever a traveler needs specific information about their river, they know they can be available for consultation.

This metaphor describes how specialization has evolved within graphic design. In most instances the specialization of these segments has become so highly refined, that they have become design businesses with their own strong self-image and marketing strategy. Many of these "marketing communications" firms add to their creative strength by combining strategic planning and research as part of their services.

Meeting the Client's Needs

These areas of specialization are important and necessary in today's complex business community. Graphic design began with and still has many firms practicing a variety of disciplines. For example, let us consider a basic business scenario. We'll assume that graphic design firm, A + B Associates has a client, The Widget Corporation. TWC (as The Widget Corporation likes to be called) believes a new logotype to promote the introduction of its new line of improved widgets will benefit TWC's product introduction as well as the corporate image. A + B Associates creates the new Widget Identity along with promotional brochures for TWC's sales personnel and customers, in-store banners, posters, counter cards, tee shirts, and buttons with the new logo for employees. It has also created the packaging system for the new Widget line that will be responsive to the needs of warehouse storage systems, as well as consumer packaging. Everything is so successful that TWC asks A + B Associates to develop an advertising program that will keep the Widget Identity firmly in place in the public's mind and complement the new design system. In addition, new dealer's sales sheets and parts catalogue are assigned to A + B Associates. It's an excellent client/design firm relationship. Every time The Widget Corporation needs anything done, they know just who to call.

That's wonderful, you say. What could possibly be wrong with this picture? Well, nothing. There are many firms that have managed to maintain this sometimes enviable diversity of work. Some of these firms are internationally famous, and many are found in smaller cities such as Seattle or Atlanta. However, the motivating factors producing the current climate of specialization have always been the forces that drive the needs of business. When business has grown to certain proportions, many large corporations have a greater comfort level choosing specialized design firms.

Let us once again, turn our attention to The Widget Corporation. Eight highly successful years have passed. TWC has increased its output and manufactures 53 different consumer products. It also has "gone public" and now is listed on the New York Stock Exchange. TWC has recently diversified by acquiring several other corporations. TWC learns that it needs to court the financial community for funding. It is through the vehicles of its annual reports and quarterly reports that TWC can position the company properly with respect to the stock brokerage houses and the banks. The Widget Corporation's Board of Directors now believes it may serve the corporation's best interests to seek out a graphic design firm that has a proven track record in dealing with the subtleties of producing such corporate literature. TWC has additionally, discovered some of its products are losing their market share in the now more complex marketplace. After a consumer research study, TWC's market research firm has recommended a new packaging system that will allow their products to be more visually competitive. TWC clearly needs a firm that understands the research studies, their value, how to interpret the visual criteria and develop a creative strategy that will distinguish TWC's product from the competition. It will seek out a graphic design firm specializing in packaging design. And when TWC comes to believe that their corporate identity system no longer is appropriate for their new position in the marketplace it seeks out a marketing communications specialist. After strategic analysis, this specialist may not only redesign the old TWC logo but recommend changing TWC's name to something that will not be identified only with widgets but also can be easily adapted to the stock market ticker quotation requirements, adding to its recognition factor.

As you can see, the age of specialization is very much with us for many functional reasons, and indeed, shows no signs of substantially diminishing. Firms that have limited their activities to certain areas of expertise discovered this limitation to be extremely advantageous to their own business. It established them as the experts who solve specific problems. Thus, their reputation grew, identifying them as having the know-how required to fulfill a client's needs, and they in turn became finer-tuned within their specialization. So the restrictiveness feeds upon itself — setting up the dictum: the more specialized work you do, the more you become expert, the more specialized work you get.

Expanding and Diversifying Services

The 1990-1993 recession has produced a movement toward firms trying to expand their product services. This response to a diminishing source of work is a logical step. Nonetheless, when expansion occurs, it is within the framework of the core business. Conversely, the many firms who had expanded their services during the 1980's to include other business profit centers and branch offices found themselves hurt by the recession. The restructuring pattern of these firms was to sell off or close down business units and return to their original core business.

With the problem solving tasks required by design firms to meet their client's marketing objectives, and our Widget Corporation as a role model in mind, we will now analyze the individual regions of graphic design with a look to the future.

Identity Design

3 **T**he core message of this survey is the fact that graphic design is a business and the various sectors of design are utilized as strategic marketing tools. The design business is unusual because its product is creative; it has no inventory. This statement requires the caveat that all business is creative. Any successful business is probably directed by a very creative, entrepreneurial and innovative individual. Most designers are so caught up in their own creative powers that they fail to recognize this reality. The particularly appealing element of the graphic design business is its output. The product of the service is creative and the quality of design is the driving force.

With recognition of the vigor and vitality of these factors influencing the business of graphic design, let's now immerse ourselves into the domain of graphic design.

The Identity Business

Identity is image. If there is one essential word we could attach to any part of graphic design or advertising, it is image. We are all in the image business in one way or another. We build and contribute value to the image of goods and services for every business imaginable. We do it through perception of the company's graphic "look" and we do it through hard or soft sell, advertising in print and various media. Identity is utilized as a strategic business tool. In graphic design it falls into three basic categories. They are:

- Corporate Identity
- Retail Identity
- Brand Identity

Corporate Identity

The methodology of corporate identity is the strategic positioning and creative impact of a company's visual image. How that firm is perceived by its clients, public, stockholders and employees is a crucial element, and CI (corporate identity) is a key marketing tool in every facet of the company's communications. The identity program affects all printed matter, advertising, building signage, trucks, uniforms, promotion materials, packaging, and any other possible conveyance of the corporate image.

Many design firms, large and small, take on identity assignments. The large and/or highly specialized firms are able to stress in greater detail the strategic planning components of corporate identity utilizing their teams of account services staff. The scope of these programs can be as small as a simple stationery system or as comprehensive as the fully realized program just described. Such a program would require intensive research and study of the corporate culture, including the firm's past, present, and future perceptions of itself. The process allows the consultant to recommend a strategy to pursue which will include evaluation of the company's name and finally its visual image. Note that the visual image is the final result of the strategic positioning, not the first step. To allow the implementation of the image, an extensive identity manual will be required.

**Phase 1
Audits**

Therefore, a sophisticated CI practice includes an intensive period of strategic planning, assessment and inventory of the internal and external operations of the corporation. This "audit" is accomplished by teams composed of account executives, project managers, planners and graphic designers, which can fluctuate, depending on the personnel available within the consulting firm. In structuring themselves as strategic consultants, some firms emphasize their staff of account services executives during this "phase 1" development period. (In some firms the creative department may be excluded from the first phase of project definition altogether.) For other companies the structure can mean the creative directors assume the account function without any other staff. These varying structures can offer a vastly different perspective to the graphic designer who tends to think of corporate identity strictly in terms of the visual image.

As a result, many large marketing communications firms have structures in which individuals employed in the marketing, sales, and account services hold significant positions within the firm and work in tandem with the creative group. While the ratio of account services to creative can be equal or even tip the balance away from creative, these firms are still creatively driven. Their own image as "Marketing Communications" consultants in this instance means operating as image and planning consultants with the visual solution to be determined and executed at the conclusion of the process.

The Audit and Phase 1 period of CI strategic planning surveys all of the corporation's existing visual materials in current operation. The audit tracks inconsistencies in the materials, perhaps inconsistencies in logotypes. It is not uncommon for large corporations to have so many divisions functioning independently that over the years the logomark, color, and type can have many variations. It produces a contradictory and disjointed visual message weakening the entire impression of the corporate image. The audit's other purpose is to analyze the internal corporate mission. It is as if the audit takes the temperature of the company. By interviewing staff at different levels, the audit learns what the firm thinks of itself, what it believes it wants to accomplish and what it believes it wants to communicate. The end result of the audit should be an extensive profile of the company, emphasizing the perception of the firm from within and from without. The Phase 1 procedure can now address the problem-solving requirements of the new and/or updated image and how to communicate this energizing message from a clear point of view.

Nomenclature

The first phase of the new or revised vision of the corporation will address the firm's name. Does the name still communicate what the consensus believes the company represents? Should the name be changed subtly or dramatically? The issue of "equity" becomes a major factor. Equity means how readily a name, its logotype, and corporate message are recognized by the public. If the recognition factor is very strong there may be less tampering with its intrinsic character and emphasis may be placed on modernization or establishing an updated look. *The protection of the equity is a fundamental consideration in any name or image change.* These are the essential questions that must be answered at this stage. Name changes are common with mergers, and mergers represent a key market for new corporate identity business. When companies are merged or acquired something, if not everything, will need to be changed.

There are some interesting examples of excellent work by the nomenclature experts, and some extremely bad choices as well. For example, Sperry Rand was a merger of the Sperry and Rand corporations. Then the name was shortened to Sperry. When Sperry and Burrows merged the result became Unysis. This name was an interesting process for it was the result of a company contest for a new name. Some names are developed in response to their symbol on the stock market. Nobody refers to IBM as International Business Machines. Citicorp was The City Bank of New York until it determined its mission was to become an international bank. These are a few corporate examples. The naming of products and the relationship to new product development dovetails with branding efforts. As new products (branding), corporations or business services are developed and introduced, their chosen name is the essential component of the recognition factor.

**Visual
Solutions**

It is only after all of these studies that the graphic designer can begin to delve into the visual systems that will create the solutions needed. Systems design is what a lot of identity design is all about. It is the operable visual systems that will bring clarity and order to the strategy of image. Another important advantage of establishing a workable solution is the cost savings to the company. The elimination of duplications in forms and printed materials often save enough money over the long run to justify much of the cost of the CI program. However, this is not the sole motivating factor in a firm's decision to take this route. The reordering of image is far more profound.

Once the system is designed, the paramount need is to implement the program with adequate quality control. If the program is not scrupulously administered by the corporation, it will eventually fall into disarray and create many of the same problems that triggered the CI program's initiation. Should the firm be large and widespread, controlling the identity program can be a full-time task. The consultant may introduce training programs for various managers within the company and will probably suggest the need for a design management director for corporate identity (if there isn't a person in place already). Often, this experience will provide CI designers a career segue to the corporate side as Design Managers. The vehicle that will control the level of standards to be maintained is the corporate identity manual.

Manuals

The manuals can cover a wide range in style and size as well. Some master manuals are composed of encyclopedic binders with sections devoted to every possible condition in which a logo system could be applied, indicating the correct and incorrect methods of application and including precise color charts. The manual is extremely explicit, containing diagrams and many visual examples of accurate methods of placing the mark or logomark onto advertisements, forms, checks, signage, brochures, and trucks. The manual may also include camera-ready typography in different point sizes. Segments of manuals can be separated out to address specific sections of the whole picture. Such segments are distributed only to those corporate divisions which will find them applicable. Some manuals use proprietary software to disseminate the required information.

Corporate identity manuals are taking the inevitable turn toward computerization. These information vehicles can be easily disseminated via computer links within a company or sectioned out as needed to specific departments. Interactive video is also coming to the fore, offering the opportunity to deliver information to clients in a technically friendly manner.

The designer's role in corporate identity is to graphically crystallize the corporate image. That image was determined through the deep introspection of the phase 1 analysis. The conclusion of a successful identity program significantly effects the general health of the corporation. The ability of graphic designer to ply his/her talent to create meaningful design systems that communicate is why this field is highly rewarded.

Retail Identity

Retail Identity (RI) works in the same manner as corporate identity and is often a part of a comprehensive CI program. In recent years, it has been separated as a specialized area because of the rise of an important and large market in specialty retailing. Initially, retail was considered just another form of CI and much of its business was (and in some cases still is) still funneled through standard CI departments. While most people generally associate to retail with shops and stores, it can also mean gas stations, banking centers, ATMs (automatic teller machine stations), and anything you would find in a shopping mall or airport

This form of identity establishes the marketing image of the retail environment (environmental design strongly dovetails and sometimes includes retail identity). It duplicates the strategic planning of corporate identity, but the specialized focus is on retail marketing. Therefore, how the retail image is designed and marketed to the public is the designer's mission. The design may start with a logotype but will extend to the layout of the environment (again, possibly working with environmental designers), banners, shopping bags, signage and packaging.

Brand Identity and Packaging Design

Branding and packaging can rarely be separated. Traditionally, many packaging design firms were only involved with the package itself. As the significance of the design's effect on the product's marketing was recognized, design firms began to participate with the total image of the product (hence, designing the brand image). For our purposes, however, let's separate the two.

Branding or brand identity (BI) simply deals with the logotype of the product. However, it is a far from simple imaging problem, for the brand equity (the same "equity" factor as discussed in corporate identity) is the most important instrument of the marketing strategy. *If that equity is to be changed, it has to be done in a manner that will not destroy, but enhance the history of that equity.* A classic example would be a study of the Coca-Cola or Pepsi-Cola logo and how each has slowly and gradually changed over the years. These visual images are part of our culture. The subtle changes are testimony to how incremental the updates are over the years and, most importantly, the need to make changes. The manner in which these changes are achieved to update an image without changing the equity of the old is the key to branding. It is estimated that a brand and package has a life span of perhaps eight years, at which point it may need to be updated. The significant word is clearly "update."

The equity of a product and name is the reputation and goodwill of that product. The equity of a corporation or product is the essential marketing tool challenging the designer. You can be sure the corporation's product managers are very cautious to protect any changes that might challenge the image's equity as revealed in the product's positioning and market share. *Graphic designers must learn the company's marketing strategy before they can begin to tamper with the design. They must be able to communicate on equal terms with the brand and product managers.* These are the classic MBA (Master of Business Administration) folk that have never taken a design course, just as designers rarely have access to marketing in their curriculum. While the problems inherent in this situation are clear (and one wonders when higher education will catch on), these two constituents are in partnership and must work as a team to bring the solutions to fruition. The graphic designer must recognize that the path to success requires communication with the marketing and business powers that be. While both designer and marketer should learn in this process, the designer must aggressively absorb the appropriate marketing language and savvy to achieve the established goals.

Packaging design has had a powerful impact on the advertising and marketing of consumer products, since it has long been recognized as the last point of communication with the consumer. Advertising's role is to condition the individual's product perception (for example, how you feel about a product). It also establishes its status and identifies its audience. Advertising can promote a product or offer incentives to buy the product. It is packaging, however, that performs the former (the product must be ready to show in

Product Equity

the ads) and latter task of presentation to the consumer.

The package communicates in advertising when an image of it is displayed in tandem with the advertising copy in print ads. However, its strongest impact is on the shelf. It is in the retailer's arena that the package must stand out against its competition. The marketing researcher's role is to control the focus groups and research studies to determine how the product is perceived and accepted by the public. Does the package (and the advertising) send the message determined by the corporate marketing and product managers? Is the color, design, size, and positioning of the branding correct? The designer's priority is to manipulate these elements to solve and precisely communicate these objectives. The package becomes a three-dimensional advertisement and it operates at the last place of consumer resistance or impulse — the crucial moment the consumer reaches for the product on the shelf.

Shelf Impact

Packaging design also consists of many technical elements that the graphic designer needs to know. There is the physical structure of the package itself. The materials, printing, and engineering are some of the elements tangential to the design. Product or industrial designers can provide the three-dimensional design needed as well as packaging engineers. In addition, the designer is currently faced with concerns about ecology, and must decide how to eliminate unnecessary boxes and how to use environmentally safe materials and printing processes. The so-called "green" movement or "green" packaging denotes an effort toward ecologically sound packaging. It is a movement that first gained momentum in England around 1989 and whose time has come. Corporations are beginning to embrace the concept, and consumer awareness of ecological needs is rising. When corporations believe "green" packaging and "green" products will generate marketing benefits due to consumer acceptance, use of such

Green Packaging

packaging and products will accelerate. It will certainly be a force in marketing and design for the future. Federal regulations are also mandating changes in packaging labeling. How the size, actual content, nutritional elements, and ingredients are displayed are under new federal scrutiny. All these factors challenge the graphic designer's ability to create a successful design that is responsive to the criteria established by the client.

Of all the divisions of graphic design, packaging design studios have perhaps experienced the most rapid computerization, and therefore the restructuring of their work force. The

Studio Computerization

Apple Macintosh environment is the market standard and design firms are on line. They are able to complete color and layout variations at a speed unknown before. They are also very successful in implementing the line extensions as required. Line extensions contain the modifications for a product's variations, such as a jam line whose label will change color with different flavors, or a shampoo that requires different labels for dry or oily; scented or unscented.

The computerization of design firms has created another, more substantive change in the emerging character of these firms which divides them into two district groups. First, firms that can manage the required strategic planning and product positioning are moving to the forefront of industry leadership. These firms' projects are the large national and multi-national brands with many SKU's (Stock Keeping Units, a count of every unit of change in a product's size or line extension, such as how many units are spun off a single product). Second, there are many small design groups, perhaps less than ten people, who work on smaller brands or less complicated projects. Computerization has made these firms fast and nimble. The pricing of projects and the demand for speed has the negative effect of turning the work of these firms into a commodity, an item that is purchased on the premise of delivery on time for the lowest price.

Packaging design has the enviable attribute of being almost recession-proof. In difficult economic times corporations may not earmark funds for research, development and new products, and they may cut back on their advertising budgets. But they do recognize that certain products will be bought, no matter what. How will they command control of the consumer at the point of purchase? Through the package. History has proven that while design firms can be downsized, they rarely let go of their prized designers. They find other ways to economize. My experience has shown there has always been a market for excellent packaging design talent.

Career Paths

Successful packaging designers develop such savvy in marketing that their career paths become quite flexible with many options. After years of apprenticeship and experience in design firms, many find their futures may include not only becoming a key player with possible equity in their firm, but the ability to transfer their skills to the corporate sector. They can assume positions within corporations in design management. Design management positions usually entail managing product lines from the creative point of view within the corporation. Design managers rarely have hands-on creative responsibilities, but rather manage the process by working in liaison with the corporation's product and marketing groups, as well as controlling the creative process by supervising design studios and vendors. Design managers must be able to make critical taste judgements, articulate marketing objectives, and work within the corporate environment. Some other designers go on from their creative responsibilities to take positions stressing strategic planning, account services or new business development. Some prefer to operate small independent design firms or to become permanent freelancers. The required skill and specialized knowledge of packaging establishes their value, whichever direction they choose.

Print Design

4 This is a vast area, attracting designers who love print. In its simplest form, print design includes any printed materials that are two-dimensional, such as pamphlets, brochures, posters and various other published materials. The semantics of the communication fields can sometimes be confusing. In advertising, "print" refers to ads—print advertising—as opposed to advertising on television or film. And in advertising, "collateral" refers to many of the projects designers call "print," such as brochures and other printed materials separate from ads.

For our purposes, the following areas are included in the context of print design.

Corporate Literature

Corporate literature is so broad it can include every and all forms of brochures, annual reports, sales tools and promotional print. It includes companies whose products may be business-to-business services, financial or technical services, or consumer products. It speaks to all sectors of the economy. Editorial design plays a role as well, as many firms have company magazines and newsletters. The field of corporate communications is dominated by the need to produce a vast variety of print materials whose audience is both within and without the corporation.

Print design has suffered in recent years the stigma of being too"design-y," that designers make things look too "pretty." Indeed, there have been many examples of design becoming so precious and so self-involved that it fails to communicate. The obsession with texture and small typography helps support the observation that some materials are illegible. The challenge is to overcome the perception that designers are only communicating with their peers. Often the public and the designer's clients become confused. Designers may have pursued a cutting-edge image but if the work didn't serve basic communication needs, the chances were the client would move on.

Information Design

Print design, like every other sector of the communications field, has to be responsive to the marketing and informational needs of the project. *Information is the operative word for whatever mode of print we discuss.* Its mission is to inform about products and communicate the image and ideas of the corporation. Information design is becoming one of the buzzwords of the 1990's as businesses consistently move toward stressing accountability and value-added services. The dissemination of clear, logical information is the challenge facing every designer in a world that is deluged with too much information to absorb. Design must confront the necessity to develop systems that deliver an understandable message. The designer must also develop the skills to analyze and conceive what the message should be. In order to achieve this goal a designer needs to be concerned with all aspects of the message, not just the visual. The designer has the ability to provide the pivotal role by recommending concept, content and strategy along with design. *Copy is the conceptual partner to the visual solution and copy is the key component with which designers must work.* In the past, copy was associated only with advertising. Not so today.

There is an old perception among advertising agency folk that designers are not conceptual. In their viewpoint, designers only know how to make things look good (and of course they know all about typefaces and computers) but they are basically not conceptual the way advertising is. The concept is not often expressed to designers, and when it is, it is greeted with understandable shock. This notion is perhaps admissible for some of the purer elements of design. It certainly is not valid for the designer who understands the value, meaning, and necessity of copy as the motivating force that sets the direction for visual interpretation. Another aspect of this parochial view is the differentiation within advertising between art and copy. While they both are integral functions of the creative, and while art directors and copywriters work as teams, advertising has traditionally been copy-driven. When an agency needs to hire a creative director, their request will often acknowledge an ambivalence as to whether the person has an art or copy background. But, in fact, when the decision-making process is over, the position usually goes to the copywriter. It's a bewildering fact to most art directors. Why does this happen? Because the message, and therefore the essential concept, is most often in the copy. The sooner art directors and designers begin to think of this total picture of integrated art and copy, the better.

Informational Design

Informational design is semantically a variant of information design, an interesting career tangent, and a combination of print design and systems design. Information systems and systems design have been applied to the design of forms, legal documents and publications stressing facts. Guide books, instruction manuals, charts, graphs, newspaper, and television informational visuals are all important regions for this work. It is a small but growing area of graphic design that offers the tremendous value of clarity in a society which is overloaded with information. It demands and requires the analysis of information and for that information to then be designed and delivered in a clear logical manner. The needs of audience must always be served and the information kept "consumer friendly."

The New York design firm Siegel & Gale opened a new frontier in graphic design when it developed Language Simplification in 1975. It came as a response to a need for clarity of business forms, both in their visual appearance as well as the written language. Alan Siegel was the first to recognize the opportunity to pair the work of graphic designers with attorneys to produce loan forms, all kinds of applications and even the redesign of federal tax forms for the United States and Canadian governments. The work has proven fascinating to designers who have an interest in combining their typographical skills with systems design, and Language Simplification has also benefited the public in a measurable way.

Others have followed the systems design approach to disseminating information and thus have developed businesses which provide visual relief to our over-crowded media environment. One such example is Richard Saul Wurman, who opened his Access Press, Ltd. in 1984 and The Understanding Business (TUB) in 1987. Both publishing efforts were designed to find solutions for information to be delivered in a visually coherent manner. Access Press started designing city tour guides but adapted the format to include guides on finance, medicine, and sports. The Understanding Business also redesigned the 80 year-old Smart Yellow Pages directories in California, and now has a host of other corporate clients.

Informational design is most appropriate for designers who thrive on analytical and organizational systems and typography. These are only a few examples and the field has yet to be fully explored. Much of this work is tangent to areas of computer design covered in Chapter 8 and these skills can also be transferred and utilized in exhibition design.

Annual Reports

This highly specialized field is another example of an area always requiring creative talent skilled to meet the needs of marketing corporate communications. The annual report is a mandated corporate year-end report and has grown into a significant marketing tool for those publicly held corporations which need to attract investors. The Federal Security and Exchange Commission mandates that all publicly held corporations issue annual reports to their stockholders. In addition many choose to issue quarterly reports.

These materials have become informational guidebooks to the corporation. They not only communicate the image and economic health of the organization, but have come to express how the organization feels about itself and its future. The

Communicating Corporate Image

annual report is significant not only because it is distributed to the stockholders, but because it is a marketing tool to the financial sector (Wall Street), to future investors and employees. It is an instrument of research for anyone who wants in-depth information on the company. The annual report can perhaps convey a story line or interviews with employees or customers. Since the report's role so strongly relies on image, it has become one of the corporation's most significant communications devices. The point of view in the written copy as well as the visual image can narrate a far more focused message than reading the mandatory financial in the back of the book. It's the company's annual opportunity to communicate its story. Even a superficial look at a random selection of annual reports will quickly reveal their vastly divergent viewpoints. A closer look will confirm that this is a highly sophisticated medium of corporate communications.

The financial information submitted by the corporation has to be scrutinized carefully for accuracy. The overriding message as well as the company's depiction has to be approved by the CEO and President. Sometimes the very nature of the annual report can trigger an overly obsessive case of collective corporate paranoia. I remember a time when a designer had to insert and remove a single comma some 15 times. The designer is in partnership with the top echelon of the firm and the whole enterprise's responsibility rests on few shoulders. It can be a tense time, with the designer in a pivotal position.

Annual reports have also come to be a design status symbol for the corporation. For some companies, much emphasis is placed on the quality of the image they wish to portray. When reports win coveted prizes, the prize goes to the corporation as well as the design firm. While the pressure exists to get the job done right and on time, the freedom to use the report as a creative medium is considerable in some cases. Huge budgets can be riding on large printings. Only the very best photographers and illustrators will do. The quality of paper and printing become paramount. These priorities can be hard to duplicate in other avenues of print design. The result is often an enviable work.

Graphic designers who work within this area can realize a meaningful and well-compensated career. The key is having the staying power, for too often there is a significant burnout factor. This is caused by tight deadlines, changes in content, delays and the fact that the majority of annual reports are **Work Place** subject to strict deadlines. Reports coincide with the **Demands** company's annual meeting and usually appear early in March. As a consequence, these deadlines produce a fairly seasonal business in which the bulk of the work is done between Labor Day and April 15th. Most firms are attempting to structure their businesses into a 12 month year. Some annuals do not have the April 15th deadline and firms are also able to develop other design products. During these deadline periods studios can work very long hours, six to seven days a week. Then there is the need to go "on press," to supervise the printing, make any last-minute decisions and make sure it is as "perfect" as possible. While press time is reserved in advance, of course there are always last-minute emergencies. It seems everyone I have ever known has ended up on press at two a.m. in some small town somewhere in the United States. You can understand why people get burned out and may want to leave this specialized field. But when you look at the really great reports, you can also understand why there are those who are totally dedicated to this work.

Corporate Communications

This identifier is usually used for corporate materials that are often, but not exclusively, accomplished by an in-house corporate staff. These are the communications products that serve to promote the corporation. They can include, but are not limited to, capability brochures, annual reports, company newsletters, sales tools, internal company forms, posters, invitations, special events, logomarks for subsidiary divisions, audio-visual materials, sales meeting materials, incentive awards, and company magazines. The communications sector of a corporation may also work with an assigned advertising agency if there is not one in-house. Few corporations do their own advertising.

Designers working within a corporation usually have a very different experience than those working for a marketing communications firm or design studio. The biggest difference is that, while the designer may have many corporate divisions as "clients," there is really only one client. This is one of those good news/bad news trade-offs. The diversity of many clients is found in design consultancies but chances are it will be a specialized consultancy. The corporation may offer only one very large client and the diversity comes from having to do virtually everything for that client.

Working for a corporation used to mean substantial job security. While that notion has changed with the economic turmoil of the last decade, the turnover in corporate positions is still much lower than in the offices of design consultants. Corporations are slower to hire and slower to fire. The atmosphere is traditionally conservative. Corporate positions are highly prized for their excellent benefit programs, shorter work weeks and relative security. Obviously, since corporations are located all over the country, the ability to relocate is a necessity.

Editorial Design

Editorial design refers to the design of magazines. The publishing field is not the only market for editorial designers, as many special interest groups and corporations will develop books and magazines as part of their corporate communications effort. It works much like other areas we have discussed, except the "client" is the publisher and/or editor. The audience is the public at large.

Publishing is, of course, the core for editorial design and it is a field in which the publishers and editors make the primary decisions relating to the focus, concept and marketing of the product. They hire the creative director and/or art directors who can work with them to visualize their publication's point of view. A creative director is usually necessary when a publication is very large or there are several publications within a group. Otherwise the top creative title is usually senior art director or art director. Under the creative head is a creative group whose size depends again on the size of the publication and how often it is published. A weekly publication requires more effort than a monthly. This group may therefore, include an associate art director, assistant art director, designers, and production artists. It is always valuable to check the mastheads of magazines, for they will credit the staff and this allows you to see the structure. The creative director or art director will be responsible for hiring the staff which can also include photo stylists or photo editors. The distinction between an art director's responsibility and a designer's is reflected in their roles. The art director "directs" the creative team on staff as well as directing photo shoots, art directing illustrators and generally functions as a person who makes creative decisions in a supervisory manner. The designer is primarily involved with the hands-on implementation of those decisions working on the layout (mostly with software programs), and perhaps makes some of the type and visual decisions. The designer's responsibilities will vary depending upon the size of the staff and how much the art director may wish to delegate. If the publication's staff is small enough, the art director may be asked to do the work of a designer as well. Designers are hired because of their ability to understand the subject matter and visually realize the magazine editor's focus. When designers change jobs it is also easier to move within a subject matter. For example, high fashion and financial based publications are so far apart in their content that most often a switch from one to the other is not possible.

Magazines fall into specialized business categories. They are:

- Life style (including regionals, such as *New York Magazine*)

- Fashion

- Business

- Trade (not found on newsstands)

- High Tech (computers, science)

- Consumer and Special Interest (computers, automotive, children, education, travel, health & fitness, entertainment, financial)

Editorial promotion is often found integrated within the editorial department. Magazine promotion can mean designing rate cards, subscription inserts, and promotional brochures and kits geared to attract advertisers. While we discuss promotion separately, it is necessary to point out how often it is closely linked with the editorial. The publisher will, of necessity, have a keen interest in the magazine's effective promotion. In addition, on small publications, the art direction staff may be called upon to design or supervise the promotion as well as the magazine.

Book Design

Book design is often perceived in relation to the design of book jackets. While this is the most visible, and in some ways splashy, manifestation of the design work, it is far from the whole story. The layout of the total book is a subject that requires insight into the character and purpose of the book. It requires establishing in the layout a sensitivity toward systems design and informational design, as well as a deep concern for typography. Often the design responsibilities will be separated, with one person responsible for the cover and another person for the interior. Art directors will originate the overall concept and then source the appropriate illustrators, photographers, and typographers to achieve their vision.

The book publishing field falls into many specialized categories as well, within the separations of hard cover, soft cover and paperback. They include:

- Text books

- Fiction/Nonfiction

- Children's publications

- Trade publications

- Special Interest (travel, cookbooks, etc.)

The computerization of publishing has created several important new directions. Within the textbook area, it is now possible to customize text-books to meet teachers' specialized requirements. Books are being designed with flexible formats so that an instructor can request a text containing specific chapters from perhaps different source books. The final customized text can be delivered on short notice and with the instructor's name on the cover.

Book Packagers

Book packagers occupy an interesting corner of the publishing field. They sometimes group publications together based on compatibility of subject matter or perhaps package a promotional device along with the book. A common example of a packaged publication grouping would be "The Collected Works of ..." More inventive packages can offer an aligned product such as the well known illustrator Geoffrey Moss' wonderful children's book "Henry's Moon" (packaged by Sommerville House in conjunction with Little Brown Publishing), which included a night light with a shade that was an illustration from the book.

Interactive Video

Publishing's utilization of new technologies is moving the field into interactive video. It is, after all, nothing more than taking existing published material and putting it on an interactive screen. The inherent qualities of the interactive process and how it involves the participant (see Chapter 7, Multi-Media / Audio Visuals) produces a wonderful learning device. How to play better tennis, visit a museum, or learn about history can be more effective in this format. It's a business that will create many new jobs for designers as each option on the screen requires another layout.

Book design positions exist primarily within publishing firms, but a large number of assignments are distributed to small studios and freelancers. The practice of creative directors or art directors to assign projects allows for the type of design flexibility required by vastly different subject matter. The sourcing of outside talent allows total design adaptability.

Environmental Design

5 This area is an amalgam of two dimensional and three-dimensional design, and so it attracts industrial designers, architects, interior designers, as well as graphic designers. It is an emerging discipline, and allows designers to work in many diversified ways, and usually with a expanded team of creative people. Environmental design represents a mosaic of design specialties, and therefore stands alone, unique in this capacity. The identifier "environmental" does not pertain to ecological concerns. This is a semantic confusion that sometimes causes the mistaken belief that an environmental designer is working on projects to clean up our environment.

A Definition

It is difficult to give a narrow definition of environmental design because it is a broadly based discipline. Many retail design and industrial design characteristics apply to this field as well, and environmental design projects attract designers from both areas. Environmental design is gaining recognition as a specialized design field as designers gain experience with the specific problems encountered in working on environmental projects. The focus of this design area is on design projects of interior and exterior spaces, often in relationship to a larger environment. Environmental designers are not architects responsible for a total structure. They can, however, work with architects to produce spaces that usually incorporate the usage of graphic design as well. A sampling of the kinds of projects that the environmental designer can administer would include: retail marketing, store planning, shopping mall design, airport facilities, hotel spaces, office building lobbies, all signage projects, parks, zoos, subways, and exhibition design.

Where Environmental Designers Work

Most positions are found in small (less than 25 people) design consultancies. These firms will usually request a specific area of involvement such as an exhibition designer or perhaps a signage designer. Nonetheless the work and skills required are quite flexible.

Corporations occasionally utilize environmental designers, most often in the retail areas (store planners, display, etc.), or in massive theme park developments (see Licensing, Chapter 6). Walt Disney's Imagineering division in Burbank, California is a premier example, employing a very large staff of environmental designers and conceptualizers who work in a thinktank environment utilizing exhibition designers, illustrators, modelmakers, graphic designers, industrial designers and signage specialists.

In addition, landscape architects are sometimes a source for signage projects. In any discussion of environmental design the relationship to industrial design and industrial design education is very important. (Please see Chapter 7, Industrial Design.)

A Sampling of Projects

Perhaps a look at the 1991 Society of Environmental Graphic Designers (SEGD) award-winning projects is a way to understand the scope of environmental design. The gold and silver awards included: The Ellis Island Immigration Museum; Topo-Graphic, Pullen Park, Raleigh, NC (a temporary landscape art installation); Jefferson High School Auditorium Lobby, Los Angeles, CA; Esprit Kid Store Prototype; and Editel Boston, Boston, MA (identity sign and canopy on exterior of building). Some of the bronze awards included the construction barricade for Cathedral Place in Vancouver; and the Signs & Information System for JFK Airport 2000.

This list indicates not only the range of the projects but also the scale. It is no wonder this area of design is gaining in recognition. Colleges are beginning to include environmental design in their curriculum and designers are becoming more enthusiastic about entering this expanding field.

Promotional Design

6 Promotion represents an exceptionally broad area, one probably least known to most young designers, and yet offers the largest number of employment opportunities. Sales promotion is also the place where design and advertising meet. Therefore an understanding of marketing strategies, copywriting and marketing communications is necessary. The promotional designer has to connect these elements to produce a printed piece that will cry out for attention and sell an idea, service, or product.

Integrated Advertising and Design

We have touched on many of the differences between design and advertising. It must be noted, however, that as the advertising world has become decentralized and more diversified, there are many firms that are true hybrids of these two disciplines. This is a new breed of agency which is generally smaller and stresses a type of problem solving that breaks down barriers and stereotypes. These companies are exciting. However, while their work will utilize and emphasize a impactful design element, in many cases it is still conceptual advertising. Other similar groups are the divisions within many large advertising agencies which are devoted to sales promotion or marketing communications. These groups require the talent of designers who can think of marketing strategies. It is an opportunity for the designer who wants the challenge of thinking on a different scale.

Some of these firms are philosophically wed to the concept of integrated marketing. *Integrated marketing* is a method of approaching a communications problem from a catholic point of view. The strategy may combine a package of various media for the client to promote his goods or services in a variety of ways. These packages may include promotional design, traditional advertising, packaging design, direct marketing or special events. Many large advertising agencies, who have subsidiary divisions, attempt to provide integrated services, but at this point in time they are just beginning to break new ground.

Sales Promotion

Although the premise is similar to advertising, it must be remembered that promotion is not print advertising. Sales promotion is printed matter that can be in the form of brochures, sales kits, sell sheets, rate cards, point-of-sale displays (POS — or sometimes called point of purchase, POP — as seen in super-markets, drug stores, banks, or any other retail establishments), banners and posters. Special promotional gifts can come in the form of kits, boxes, special events marketing and sales giveaways, such as kits, tee shirts, buttons, matchbooks, hats and menus or contests, sweepstakes and other incentive offerings (special mailers, posters, and displays). Within the publishing field we can find special inserts in magazines (for subscriptions, mail-aways), magazines advertorials (multi-page editorial inserts sponsored by an advertiser). Many package goods companies will offer free standing inserts (F.S.I.'s are coupons, often part of an ad, inserted in newspapers and magazines). Outdoor promotions include billboards and posters on mass transit or bus shelters. The cosmetic and fragrance market has made special promotions of gift-with-purchase and purchase-with-purchase (GWP and PWP as they are prevalently known) a way of life in department stores. They also utilize special mailers distinct from, but sometimes similar to, direct marketing advertising.

Promotional Firms

As you can see, promotion covers a vast area. The products promoted can include anything that is marketed throughout the world. This accounts for its huge diversity. To understand how broad-based promotion is, apply these items (all of which have to be designed) to the diversity of companies needing these services. Think about all the sales promotion generated by an IBM. The product categories; sales tools for sales personnel; giveaway information for the consumer; trade shows for marketers and retailers with their trinkets of balloons, pens, and discs; the retail outlets' need for display cards, posters, signage; the promotions for a charity or cause (fund raising, ecology, etc.); the awards given to distinguished personnel (gift and travel incentives, as well as trophies and awards); and materials for corporate sales conventions (programs, name tags and menus). Now consider what it might be like handling the promotion for a television network: developing sales kits to promote sponsorship of specific programs (promoting the time buying); attracting affiliate stations to airing specific shows (which are "leased" from the network); or creating consumer awareness (on-air promotional spots). If you were working for a fragrance/cosmetic company you would develop many of these same products but with a completely different image and point of view.

The diversity is enormous and underrated as an avenue for career opportunities. I've often felt sales promotion is an unknown field in the minds of young designers, for it certainly has a very low recognition factor. It may not be the most glamorous design work, but it can be a lot of fun and does offer a significant number of employment opportunities.

Where Are the Promotion Jobs? Promotion can be produced by design studios as well as in-house corporate groups. Most publishing firms devise a large sales promotion effort. The balance between design done within a company and the amount given to outside studios or agencies is a pendulum whose swings are dependent on the economic times and mood. Many advertising agencies have traditionally had sales promotion groups within the agency.

When they are part of the internal structure of the agency they work for the same clients as the agency. The agency does the print advertising, radio and television. The promotion group does anything else required by the client, from packaging design to cookbooks. Many of these groups have been spunoff as separate profit centers, perhaps with different names that may or may not be directly associated with the agency name. These spin-offs occur to allow the promotional group to seek clients different from the parent company without causing a conflict of client interests. For example, an agency might have a banking client, which would prevent them from working for another financial institution. However, a separate promotional design group could pitch other financial services client, promoting their expertise in that area. Advertising agency promotional groups are, in many cases, the "diversified studios" that many designers desire. The downside is that often the quality of design produced by many agencies is mediocre. While some agency sales promotion divisions do exceedingly fine work, the general level is below that of design firms. Perhaps this is explained by the general agency business focus of producing work for television spots. Promotion has traditionally been a "stepchild" department. As these groups now are becoming more attractive profit centers and the focus shifts, the quality should improve. The key to quality is determined by the quality of the client and what the client demands, regardless of where the work is done.

Licensing

This area of design has expanded greatly in the past few years and offers a whimsical, fun side to graphics. Its essence is close to the thinking behind sales promotion. Producing products with images to promote a personality or idea dates back to ancient times. While the Romans sold souvenirs at gladiator fights but no one could foresee the ubiquitous effect of sports and entertainment marketing in this century. Today the team identifying logos and mascots for the National Football League or National Basketball Association, as example, have generated a complex and multi-billion dollar industry. The marketing gurus have discovered that almost anything can be sold with a famous character or slogan such as Garfield, Batman, The Simpsons or "I Love New York" (which has spawned an industry of copied promotions). I often think of Mel Brooks nailing this subject on the head in his movie "Meatballs." In a scene discussing how the movie they are making can be merchandised before it's even made, Brooks unveils a table filled with samples of merchandising products such as Meatballs the Sweatshirt, Meatballs the Towel and Meatballs the Toilet Paper. They will guarantee the movie's success. Unfortunately, he didn't think of including a Meatballs Pavilion at a Meatballs Theme Park.

Theme Parks

Theme parks and the expansion of this entertainment related environment into restaurants, fast food chains and shopping malls have developed a further outreach of the licensing program into the creation of a total fantasy environment. The surroundings are a complete escapist world in which the consumer enters a habitat offering experiences which foster the desire to buy some object in order to retain the memory of the experience. It's fun, expensive and big business. These enterprises are a source of employment to graphic and industrial designers as well as architects, illustrators and planners. Every facet of these parks require graphics, products and environmental design. The Disney Imagineering group is famous for developing this work genre but there are several others.

The phenomenon of licensing promotion exploded in the 1980's and has produced a expanding industry mainly catering to team sports and cartoon characters. Licensing can also include fashion designers lending their names to fragrances and accessories. In fact any famous personage, brand, city, country, or entertainment vehicle is ripe for exploration or exploitation, depending upon your viewpoint. Nonetheless all these products and their accompanying logos need to be designed and so offer interesting avenues of employment. The significant factor in all this activity is the growing demand for a sophisticated product. Quality of design is an integral part of much that is produced. The graphic designer's input and imagination has moved this industry to the higher ground. The branding of these images is the motivating strategy, so that Mickey Mouse, The Muppets, Peanuts and NFL (National Football League) teams, to name a few, are becoming marketable brands. The branding phenomenon moves the images or characters far beyond their sometimes humble origins and the branding produces a perception of the consumer that they are "buying into" the essence of what the character represents.

Branding

The branding function creates products and merchandising systems every bit as sophisticated as merchandising a designer fragrance. The image (i.e. design) of the product must be appropriate to the marketplace. Accessories, home furnishings, and clothing are sold to all age and economic groups. The 1990 Disney Consumer Product catalogue included over 14,000 items, in these categories: apparel and toys (the two largest categories); home furnishings, paper goods (including greeting cards and stationery) and gifts and collectibles. They can be found in mass market and upscale retailers such as K-Mart or Bloomingdales as well as retail outlets devoted just to the brand itself (and the store becomes a environmental design project). A watch can cost $12.95 or thousands of dollars.

Corporate Licensing

Licensing has also expanded to the corporations, who are applying their image to incentive or consumer products, in a desire to proliferate the branding of their corporate identity. It is an interesting mixture of image and marketing when catalogues are offered with company logos adhered to mugs, jewelry, luggage etc. Apple computers, Aetna Insurance, and American Airlines offer a broad range of products to consumers and employees. The inherent differing nature of these corporations also offer insight as to how divergent the corporate image can be and still adapt itself to this marketing arena.

It is important to be observant and to analyze all that you see as you are a member in our society. Consider what development and design is behind these products the next time you see one on the marketplace. Remember their purpose and that graphic designers are employed for the creation of the design impact.

Industrial Design

7

his survey of Industrial Design (ID) is directed toward its relationship with graphic design. While industrial design is a discipline unto itself, no discussion of Graphic Design would be complete without considering the alliance of the two.

ID: A Cornerstone in the Evolution of Graphic Design

The origin of Industrial Design in the 1920's has been glamorized by larger than life figures who gained much media attention. Raymond Lowey, Donald Deskey, and Henry Dreyfuss were true renaissance men who integrated many facets of two- dimensional and three-dimensional design. Lowey, somewhat like Frank Lloyd Wright, was famous for his personal charisma, his vision of design's role in our culture, and as his ability to attempt any kind of project. His fame defined the classical American designer. He was responsible for the design of locomotives, automobiles (the Studebaker), corporate identity (Exxon), packaging (Lucky Strike cigarettes), housewares, and china dishes. Lowey's designs had a profound effect in shaping the look of modern-day life at the middle of this century. Industrial design took on an aura similar to Architecture (often called the mother of all the arts) and certainly was instrumental in moving the idea of graphic design forward as a profession.

Current ID Practices

Today ID has developed into a profession dominated by small scale design firms that can still control an unusual array of diversified assignments. While ID's focus is primarily three-dimensional as opposed to graphic design's two-dimensional base, the Industrial Designer can still have a significant graphic involvement. Sometimes the firm or individual will do it all, or sometimes opt to work in tandem with graphic designers.

In fact, ID most often encompasses product design and product development. The graphic component is utilized in relation to the product and is often applied graphics. Product development can, because of its intrinsic nature, require or spin off into full-blown identity programs. The products naturally can be anything and everything consumers use, from disposable to durable products. This includes the design (but not engineering) of transportation vehicles (cars, planes, bikes, motorcycles); consumer products (bottles, jars, containers); durable and "white" products (refrigerators, coffee makers, small electrical, household products, eyeglasses etc.); scientific equipment and instruments (computers, medical and surgical products, instrumentation panels, testing devices); housewares and tabletop (dishes and giftware, cookware, eating utensils); and furniture.

All design work of this nature relies heavily on the training and ability to understand human factors (the guidelines for products being used by the human body, the ergonomic requirements of a product that is reflective of human needs as pioneered by Henry Dreyfuss) and the designer's pro-active role in research and development. Industrial designers are often charged by their clients with the developmental problem solving required to establish a new product, or they may initiate and create new product ideas based on their own observations. The R & D (research and development) aspect to ID is truly innovative design not experienced in many other design disciplines.

The applied graphics on ID projects are an inherent part of the complete design program. Often the industrial designer will create all the two-and three-dimensional design. The two-dimensional components of three-dimensional projects are most often realized in identifying or decorative graphics, signage and exhibition design. It is common practice for industrial design or exhibition design firms to hire graphic designers to work as part of the design team or form co-op ventures with graphic design firms.

A survey of industrial design projects which would incorporate graphic design would include the following:

Product Design

Products frequently need graphics. Sometimes graphics are instructional or informational. Sometimes they are purely decorative. Computers, medical or telecommunications instruments require labels, numbers, buttons, instructions, and general typographic information. Sporting equipment, clothing and accessories have become graphically decorative. For example, consider the aerodynamic graphics on the clothing used by teams in the 1992 Winter Olympics. This purely graphic impact contributed an altogether new dimension to visual impression of the sporting event. And the revolution started by Swatch in watch design challenged a whole industry to seek new graphic dimensions for product design. Often when these graphic solutions unite with the name of the product, we enter the world of licensing as well (i.e. Nike sneakers, Head skis, NFL clothing and accessories, Mickey Mouse watches).

Environmental Design/ Exhibition Design

Retail environments, public spaces, trade shows, museums, special exhibitions, and corporate shows are the venue for this work. The three-dimensional planning and graphics cannot be separated. The graphics in exhibitions often require an editorial feel or point of view for they tell a story. Museums devoted to history encompass time lines (Ellis Island, The Rock & Roll Museum, and The Johnstown Flood, for example). See Chapter 5, Environmental Design.

**Multimedia/
Audio Visuals**

Within this genre of work lies the input of the A/V specialist. In the past slide projectors were routinely utilized to help tell the story. Today our technology allows for more sophisticated solutions. Interactive video is the most popular new technology with virtual reality representing the next breakthrough medium. Interactive video empowers the observer to play a proactive role in choosing paths and directions of exploration. For example, an exhibition will show a demonstration of Pompian architecture by allowing the viewer to look at floor plans of a building, then make selections on touch sensitive video screens as to which rooms to visit and which walls in those rooms to view. By pressing selections, you can move through the house, observing and learning the history of various artworks at your own pace, concentrating on individual points of interest. Computers can now be spoken to as well as touched (keyboard or on screen) to signal the viewer's wishes.

Virtual reality will accelerate the viewer's participatory role. In VR the participant dons a helmet or goggles that encompass the total visual experience blocking out any "real world" peripheral vision. The individual is visually submerged into an artificial landscape. A glove is fitted with micro processors that permit the viewer to point his or her way though the territory screened on the goggles. Thus the participant controls the choices and moves through the artificial environment as part of that environment. Applications of VR exist in training programs for the military, programs that simulate flight or combat, and in architectural or engineering programs which allow a type of immersion into a CAD system. Its future in graphic design applications have yet to be determined.

In each of these multimedia examples the dynamic of the process is changing, making the participant a proactive part of the "exhibition" instead of a passive observer.

A/V work has also meant business meetings, conventions and conferences. These meetings and seminars can be relatively small affairs requiring simple charts and graphs or extremely elaborate "special events" utilizing sophisticated technical projections, music (sometimes original), theatrical lighting, stage sets and current state-of-the-art stage craft. At this point these meetings become industrial shows which are famous for presenting all the talent that money can buy. Entertainment personalities from TV, movies or the stage are found participating with choreographers, composers and directors of equal talent. It's a form of pure "show biz" and the graphic designers have learned to function within this realm.

Special Events can also include much of the same talents as listed above devoted to some charitable event. Corporations sponsor fund raisers and utilize their in-house design staff to provide the invitations, menus, banners, decorations and any other graphic component needed.

Signage

The development of sign systems found in airports, shopping malls, hospitals, office buildings, zoos, mass transportation, and the like require a special group of skills. (This subject correlates to the work of environmental designers, see Chapter 5) The designer needs to be highly organized with a strong ability to analyze and structure information while having a love and commitment to typographic and graphic systems (graphic design). The designer also needs to know manufacturing materials and three-dimensional structural elements (usually stemming from an ID education). Lastly, the designer has to be able to draw and read drafting plans (architectural drawings). The recognition of these unique skill combinations clears the path to understanding why signage designers can, and do, develop from all three disciplines.

Signage designers are a special folk who derive much pleasure from their ability to work within a fully integrated design environment. These projects, by their nature, require the collaboration of architects, store planners, industrial designers and graphic designers. It is an interesting milieu.

The Graphic Design Connection

To recap this short survey of industrial design, I should point out how industrial design functions as an occupation with interconnecting bonds to graphic design. The relationship between the two disciplines has had several developments beneficial to graphic design. Initially ID pointed the way for graphic design to be recognized as a discipline unto itself. The development of ID as a profession has also provided a guide and model toward establishing graphic design as a recognized profession. However, at this writing, graphic design has not achieved that status. It is a complex question of accreditation and licensing. Architects must be licensed by the state in which they practice. Industrial Designers are not licensed, but through their membership in the Industrial Design Society of America, attach IDSA after their name. This signifier denotes a level of professional acceptance and elevates the individual in the public and client's eye, much the way architects will attach AIA (The American Institute of Architects) after their names. Graphic design has no equivalent practice.

In presenting the alliance between these two disciplines it is interesting to observe how these design careers can merge. Quite often industrial designers find their life's work ends up as graphic design. Some of the motivating forces are the sheer quantity of graphic design projects available compared to the much smaller industrial design business arena. While ID represents an important, integral discipline in the large scope of design, there are fewer industrial designers, fewer firms and, naturally, fewer positions. And, of course, the transition from ID work to graphic design is fairly simple because of the breadth of ID education. It is harder for the graphic designer to function as an industrial designer. To do so usually requires an intense involvement with design in the third dimension or enrolling in an ID program.

Computer Graphics

8 Today most businesses are technologically driven and therefore share the common caveat that anything written about the latest innovations is obsolete possibly at the time of writing and certainly by the time of publication. With that statement as a premise, it is easy to understand how attempting any current appraisal of the state of the art is intimidating. The designation "current time" must be in recognition of a constant state of flux. The impact of these technological influences on graphic design firms is not a recent thing, however, and while it may always be changing, we now have enough perspective to view its impact with some clarity.

A Short History of a Short History

The utilization of computers began in design firms only about ten years ago. The introduction of this technology has caused alternating confusion, acceptance and denial. Our experiences with the computerized design environment is so brief in time and so profound in scope that the challenge of how the individual will dominate the machine is still being questioned. We obviously must be creatively dominant, but many echo the fear that the seduction of instant gratification is changing the way we think and design—but not for the better. As we shall see, traditional skills are not lost and need to be retained.

Within the last six to eight years computers have increasingly become an indispensable tool; a presence moving from the single unit at a shared table to their ubiquitous presence at each designer's desk. The drop in initial costs (as with most new electronic equipment) has greatly contributed to this proliferation. At this point a fully- equipped studio with individual access to current technology is the standard.

During the mid to late 1980's our requests for hiring would call for computer experience as a plus factor in the decision making process. In other words, if a designer had some

Macintosh literacy they were way ahead of the pack and most often knew more than the person doing the hiring. By 1990 the tables had completely turned. It is now the norm to not only demand the experience on the computer, but on specific software as well. Another aspect to this transformation is that young designers will not take jobs with firms that are not technologically current. These designers feel that lack of access to up-to-date equipment will hamper their careers in the long term. And they are right! It's clear the computer (and it's the Mac environment that is standard) has assumed its dominant place within the graphic design studio.

Today's Workplace

While the importance of computer proficiency is a foremost consideration, and we shall discuss the differing functions where computer design is pertinent, we should not lose sight of its role as a tool. One of my clients stated the issue well. He said he wanted designers who were computer proficient but not computer dependent. The designer's creative choices are sometimes swayed in a particular direction based on their ability toward achieving instant gratification or certain visual and typographic "tricks." The software currently available is very seductive, and surely this condition will only accelerate. Nonetheless, designers must continue to rely on all their skills and all available tools.

Much to the surprise of many designers immersed in this revolution, drawing continues to be very important. Drawing continues to be the base of all visual communication. It is both the point of initial inspiration as well as demonstrating sensitivity and nuances not duplicated by any other means. The computer has not destroyed the importance of drawing, just as mass manufacturing has not destroyed (and maybe increased the appreciation of) hand crafts. Colleges have responded by including computer courses as a part of the requisite curriculum without discarding (and in some cases re-initiating) traditional skills such as the letterpress (a fine arts print press process in which paper is selected, type is hand-placed, hand-inked and run through the press).

In this climate of change and transition, the paths that firms seek, the roles designers play, and the challenges that need to be met create brain teasers for the best professionals. Everyone is groping and feeling their way through the maze, but since it's such a fast-moving terrain, few have the luxury of time.

Some Professionals' Opinions

One viewpoint is aptly described by Kenneth Cooke, the worldwide Creative Director of Siegel & Gale: "...the computer allows the designer to edit, retouch, set type and master many trades. This was not true 10 years ago." Ken thinks classical forms are important again. A designer should be able to draw a logo and not send it out to a lettering specialist. The economies in charge endorse the use of computer production time, offering the firm a large profit margin. The machines definitely pay for themselves and generate income. As a result everything is kept in-house and charged as out-of-pocket expenses. Offices therefore become more full-service. Designers need to know a lot more about a lot more things. They have to be knowledgeable in the state of the art (technology), know the best sources for illustration and photography and understand the business focus. The net effect to the designer is the ability to be freed from production, freed from time-consuming detail and have more time for concept work.

I asked Tom Weisz how he interprets the designer's role in the computerized workplace. Tom is a Creative Director who has demonstrated a long-term devotion to the technological cutting edge. In 1984 Apple Computer made his former design firm, Weisz and Yang (with partner Larry Yang), into an Apple "test kitchen." According to Tom, "Today the designer's vocabulary should include audio, video, animation, three-dimensional rendering and evermore complex inter- activity. Individuals will demand communication materials with information that will satisfy their particular interest. They will pick and choose what they want by pushing a button or simply asking for it. The device will answer in words and images — whether moving or still — instanta- neously. The viewer will have access to enormous amounts of information and will access that information in many new ways. It will become the professional designer or commu- nicator's role to provide that information in ways that will be exciting and of interest to the recipient."

The computerized workplace shows other indications of this revolution. The movement toward quicker, faster work patterns and clients expecting project turnaround in an unprecedented short time period has added certain dangers to

The Commodity Challenge

the field. Some small studios which cannot provide strategic planning as an integral part of the creative process may find themselves so computer-driven that they become a technologi- cally up-to-date version of production houses, providing a commodity and not a design service. The business climate is pushing toward faster and therefore cheaper. Since design firms charge clients a service fee based on billable hours, the time spent and the hourly charge of the person becomes the standard as to how much is charged later. As projects are completed in shorter periods of time due to advanced technol- ogy, design firms must find a way to protect themselves and the way the fees are structured. It presents a profound chal- lenge to many companies. Many firms, reversing this trend, have senior level personnel producing the finished work on computer. This is a waste of creative talent, resented by the designers, but passes the higher rate of billable hours to the client. Neither direction produces a satisfactory solution.

Tom Weisz comments, "Many of today's processes, while using computers, are not helping creative people to work more creatively, but are making creative individuals enslaved to the production process. Creative individuals must strive to change this by becoming more proactive in this communication revolution. Only by helping to shape this new medium will the process favor the creative individual."

Another aspect of the movement to marry the production and the creative is the development of new company relationships. Some pre-press production companies are anticipating a move towards providing a complete "turnkey" service by merging their technical expertise with creatively-driven firms.

Electronic Linkage

With the new ability to function through electronically linked locations, modems and faxes have transformed the need for workers to be grounded in a specific locale. This is surely a significant manifestation of the changing computerized workplace. Firms are decentralizing and so are their employees. Women in particular are benefiting as they can work at home, remaining with their young families, and modem their work to the design firm. The electronic linkage factor will probably have a substantial future impact as firms will be able to communicate with their clients, employees, and production output facilities through their computer networks. We are currently observing firms in New York on-line with facilities in the Far East, connected by satellite, issuing original design information and printing instructions.

At this time there seems to be two dominant structural directions the electronic design office. First, the computer has virtually replaced traditional production methods and, while graphic designers may be working directly on the computer, the technical finish is being provided by computer graphic artists. The other direction utilizes technology for new, innovative creative mediums. Both of these occupational directions are separate from the traditional graphic designer who is simply utilizing another tool at his or her disposal.

Rita Armstrong's Guide to Computer Jobs

Rita Armstrong heads my firm's computer graphic design placement department. Rita has to respond to the daily business demands for computer talent and to advise our candidates on career directions. In this quickly-changing business environment she also advises clients as to how to structure their firms to integrate personnel responsible for technology or develop computer design departments. As she is "on line" and can speak to your immediate and long-term goals, I've asked her for her perspective. Here is what she has to say to those trying to carve out a career direction in this sometimes confusing arena:

The Dilemma

"So what are you, a Computer designer, or a Computer Guru, or a production person who has a knack for laying out other's designs on the MAC?"

Answering the above question is a serious problem and a direct result of the Mac revolution. It is not just the designer or design student who needs to address this question, the employer goes through a similar quandary, asking himself, What do I need? Maybe someone who can design and produce finished mechanicals on the computer...or do I just need a mechanical artist to take either hand drawn roughs or ideas cleanly worked up on the screen through to production. When you are involved in a job search that includes computer skills, the very fact that employers don't always know what they need can work for or against you.

The old saying " to thine own self be true" is the best advice. If you would be happy overseeing the whole computer network at a design studio, as well as designing, fine, but realize that you will spend 50% to 70% of your time either answering questions about the computer, or trouble-shooting. When you go on an interview or even design your resume, take note of how much you stress your computer experience. I'm not saying to downplay your technical skills, I'm just saying if designing is your priority, than make sure that is clear. I have too many people who call me because they have become typesetters instead of computer designers. This only becomes a problem if you stay in that position for too long before realizing that it is never going to change. All at once all the work in your portfolio is someone else's design. Soon you are going to be hard to market as a designer.

The flipside also holds true. If you have a weak portfolio, but great computer skills, you may very well be able to take a computer position that gives you some design responsibilities. This kind of spot can help you slowly but surely grow into a more creative job by providing you with printed work for your book. Your best bet is to look at small design firms with less than five Macs. Small shops have a tendency to utilize every skill a person has. If the designers are overloaded they are more likely to come to you for small projects. Large corporations and agencies are less likely to hand over projects. They have specific needs and large workloads that tend to lead them into pigeonholing people.

Designer or Computer Artist?

Probably the hardest job I have is telling someone their portfolio is just not competitive enough for the design market. In other words not all books measure up to the other portfolios that are submitted for the same job. You need to know what you are up against. The smart design graduate goes to other school's portfolio reviews. In most cases, schools have open houses for graduates to show their work. Go with a friend or anyone whose work you respect. Be honest with each other as to how the work stacks up against the competition. If it doesn't look good, get a second opinion from an instructor you trust. Remember, computer skills are a necessity now, but design quality is still what studios are looking for when filling design positions. Strong computer skills can offer you another option. You may approach a small studio with your technical skills on the production side with the understanding that they will give you design responsibilities in time. Remember it will take time before they trust your skills enough to give you full design control. I've seen many junior computer designers lose faith too soon after joining a studio. It could take the young assistant up to a year to be trusted with design projects. During that time, keep up freelance work and pro bono work that you can show them. You'll gain their respect and trust.

Where Do You Fit?

The question of where you fit in has to be addressed and answered by you. You have to be honest with yourself and have the patience to figure out which route will give you the best career. Which path will offer you the best salary if that is important to you, or which will make you want to get up and go to work each day. The advent of computers has in some ways offered more options, and in other ways made the meaning of certain job titles a little muddier. Some assistant art directors I know only work on computer mechanicals. Others work on 50% follow-through and 50% design. One assistant I know makes over $40,000 and has the responsibilities of a project manager because of his computer skills. After you have made your decision, be very careful to make sure your employers have also made up their minds as to what they are looking for in you.

What Are You Walking Into?

Whether you are just starting out, or have been in the field for a while, it is a good idea to get a written job description from a prospective employer. Not only does it give you a clear idea of what is expected of you, it also is a process an employer should go through before making a hire. It allows them to take stock of what skills are necessary and in what order of importance. It allows you to see what software they are currently using and which seems to be the most commonly used. Too many employers interview candidates with the idea that they will "know what I want when I see it". This leaves too much left unsaid at interviews and allows the employer to get away with not addressing the negatives. The interview becomes an audition and the candidate is left without any solid ideas of what is expected of him or her.

After you have determined what you are or what you want your future to be, make sure that your employer is committed to the technology. Are the budgets big enough to keep the system growing? Does the person interviewing you have a computer on their desk that actually gets used? Whether you are a designer or a production artist, you don't want to get stuck in a firm that still uses PageMaker when the world is using Quark. Recently one of my candidates included the fee for the Mac Expo as part of his sign-on package. This let him find out whether the company that wanted to hire him, was also interested in supporting the technology during his employment. They informed him that they could only send one person and, while he might be the logical person to go, the Vice President usually went to the Expo. He turned down the position.

Promises, Promises, Promises

If a company wants to bring you on staff to help set up a Computer System, make them put it in writing. Find out if they will give you the tools to be successful, before you agree to join them. If they haven't already hired someone to access their needs, ask if you might be hired as a consultant first to determine what hardware and software they should invest in. Write up a proposal including how much several methods would cost. Find out what budget they would approve for equipment and software before becoming a part of the team.

If they already have this information, ask if you might review their proposal. You may find out the consultant they hired has some ties to software companies that clouded his or her view. In any case, know what you are walking into. Too many people find themselves constantly fighting the bean counters after they have taken the position. They are hired and then left to watch the slow, pitiful, frustrating, death of the computer department. They can't get the tools they need in order to take the system to a point where it pays for itself and begins to make money. Soon they are looking for another job with a failure on their resume.

What's Hot and What's Not

So who is in demand? Several areas have been showing an amazing amount of growth during what is considered to be a depressed market. There is a very strong need for packaging computer gurus at every level. Small design firms as well as corporations are upgrading their systems and need the technical expertise to make their investments worthwhile. Computer graphic managers especially are hot. I'm not referring to over-priced computer jockeys either. These are people who know the traditional pre-press process and how to implement computer mechanicals too. They know how to juggle computer time and how to determine who has the skills to complete the project quickly and properly.

Trained computer packaging production people are also in demand. Quite a few people claim to know software, but seem to get lost working on line extensions and back panels. Packaging is a rather complicated mixture of scanned images, drawn artwork, and type. It utilizes quite a mixture of software knowledge (as well as a good dose of patience for print-outs).

Small Studios

In small design boutiques the evolution of computer use has produced a whole new position, sort of a "junior network manager." Small studios may have started out with one or two Macs mainly for typesetting, but now find they have five or six and maintenance has become almost a full-time job. These managers are there to answer such questions as: Who troubleshoots when the mouse isn't moving anything on the screen or overload has caused it to crash? How much memory do we need to run? Who cleans up the files and saves them? How different is the color on my monitor from what can be expected on print? Who is going to keep us updated on what is happening out there? And the common complaint, "I'm busy pitching business and I don't have time..."

Production Job Demand

As for those interested in computer production — you are in demand! Salaries may have leveled off, but the demand is out there. These positions can pay anywhere from $20,000 to $45,000 depending on experience and management responsibilities. These positions require a knowledge of printing techniques and the ability to troubleshoot on the system. Any network knowledge will make you worth more money. Production spots include both pre-press art production and print production. There are needs for production managers with hands-on film knowledge, studio network managers, and senior and junior mechanical artists as well.

Corporations

Corporate in-house design studios need skilled people who can work with a pre-existing template for corporate magazines and newsletters. Sometimes writing and photography skills are also used in these types of positions. They are excellent spots for people who like to work independently and utilize some design skills. The computer has also changed the marketing and presentation departments in large corporations. The advances made in persuasion software have truly affected corporate presentation design. It is cleaner looking, more interesting, and often in color. Software advances have made these positions more interesting to work on as well as look at. If you have skills in juggling numbers and representing figures in an interesting manner this may be a career specialty for you to investigate. USA Today offers a good example of the quality one can achieve in presentation design on computer. These positions pay well and offer good benefits (see Chapter 9, Benefit Packages).

Agency Needs

Advertising Agencies are still sorting out what to do with computer production people. Traditionally, the production people were located and concentrated in big bullpens which functioned as a service center to the agency. Slowly but surely they have been adding Macs. The big ad agencies have been forced into investing in the technology by their clients who see it as a cost-cutting measure. This change has required more of their creative staff to become fully Mac literate. The format that seems to be the most successful is utilizing one Mac literate within a creative team, as well as keeping a fully-equipped bullpen. This is an interesting spot because the junior acts very much like an assistant art director, but, in comparison, may have a little less creative input on the project. These junior/assistant art directors often may have been moved up from the bullpen. Again this provides someone with a less competitive book the opportunity to work closely with creative talent and be involved in the design process.

Direct Mail

Direct mail is one of the hottest test areas right now because it offers the agency's clients the most "bang for the buck." You could not find a better medium for the use of computer design and production. The growth of these two together in the last decade was rather predictable. Direct Mail requires the ability to manipulate type and images in a small format cheaply and effectively. DM design must also offer a format that can easily be repeated as part of a series in a campaign. The computer accomplishes all of this very efficiently. It also reduces mechanical manpower therefore allowing a full series to be designed cheaply and quickly.

Think about what you receive in the mail, before you throw it out or please them with a response. Look at the layout, the type, and general format. It requires an editorial sense as well as advertising savvy. This might be another career direction for you to consider.

So, a friend of yours is willing to teach you IBM computer skills... Is it worth your time? Yes! Any computer experience is a welcome addition to your resume. Occasionally we have computer jobs that are quite difficult to fill because they require IBM skills. (I can also add that all job descriptions, irrespective of hardware, require an excellent design sense.) Any computer experience teaches you how to formally deal with technology. It shows you how to maneuver your way through software. Your experience will consist of making mistakes and solving them and no matter what the hardware, that kind of experience is worth your time.

Hardware/ Software

The Macintosh is, of course, the dominant system. What software should you know? This area is in constant flux. As new programs are introduced and adopted the requirements change. An example is the manner in which Quark has supplanted Pagemaker. Currently my clients want to hire Quark experts who have strong knowledge of at least one other program. In most cases, they are using Adobe Illustrator and/or Freehand. Some familiarity of Photoshop and scanning techniques is always a plus.

The New Frontiers

Whole new job titles exist because of software development. Companies that design software have become a little more sensitive to their audience's needs. In other words, Designers want well-designed software formats. Icons need to be more clear, more graphic in substance... Screen designs need to be concise, but interesting in an editorial fashion. Most of all, programs need to respond almost intuitively to what might be a designer's next choice. That means software companies and small programming boutiques are hiring designers to assist in product development. They can only learn so much from their beta testers. They need consistent access to a designer who can answer their questions and offer options. In most cases the designer works in a think tank situation along with engineers and human factors people. Only a designer can tell you how difficult indexing was on Pagemaker or why they needed it to be more flexible. A designer would know what comes next, or if a particular symbol is misleading.

I find that signage designers do well in computer software development because they are not only experienced computer users, they understand symbols and icon development. Just as they know how to give directions, they know how to move someone through a program. They apply their way-finding design techniques to the computer program.

The other area that has truly expanded and created a new design demand is multimedia. Agencies and audio visual agencies have seen the future and it starts with MacroMind director. This software program is still clumsy, but it is an affordable beginning. With it, ad agencies can move a client through a storyboard with options. Museums, schools and corporations are very interested in expanding their use of this medium. Recently a client introduced me to their latest recruiting visual on laptop. While the prospective college recruit waited for his/her interview, they had the option of viewing an interactive program on the company. It was impressive to say the least.

Interactive computer design is an exciting field. To be successful, it takes a keen interest in disseminating information in a visually pleasing manner. The technology can't get in the way of the potential user or the program will go unused. The designer should have a background in either editorial or information design, extremely strong skills on the computer, and the ability to stick to a project for an extended period of time. The companies that create these programs are structured in two ways. They may have a creative director who sketches what he is looking for, and hands over the concepts to computer designers to embellish, or they may hire designers who directly design formats with the help of an engineer.

The advent of the computer has created new challenges and new opportunities. The best weapon against getting lost in change is knowing about it before it happens. Keep as up-to-date as you can on what the technology has to offer. The computer is a tool, it will never replace people's ability to dream and design. It can only broaden our horizons and help us animate those dreams, so that they become vivid for those with whom we share them."

— Rita Armstrong

A Perspective for Now and the Future

As stated, these changes and challenges can be difficult to comprehend when there is little perspective and we are in the midst of the transfiguration.

As Tom Weisz points out, "Today's graphic designer or communication professional has the opportunity of a lifetime if they recognize their process is likely to change and they are adaptable to that change. We are at the door to a whole new world in communication. New challenges are emerging and change is the most difficult thing to ask of anyone.

The designer of our time is faced with immense pressure. Each creative individual has an enormous task at hand trying to work within this challenging new world. The creative field needs to look at itself and develop new methods that are beneficial to creative processes and procedures."

While the future may be foggy, certain truths are evident.

The technology is being harnessed and the designer has to assess his or her role as the arbiter of design and taste. The seductive nature of software will have to become secondary to the creative thought process, and only there to provide a wonderful freedom. The shifting directions of responsibilities in the work-place, as well as the very structure of that workplace, may seem confused, but after all, change always has existed as a function of life. It is a fabulous time to be creative.

I have no doubt that the creative mind will always triumph. The value and product of our creativity produced the technology in the first place. *These machines are only the result of our intellect and surely are no match for our minds.*

Getting Started:
How Do You Get There?

9

Starting a job search can be a daunting and sometimes intimidating process. It should be comforting for the novice to know that the experienced professional faces the same challenges and, while for the seasoned designer the ground rules may be familiar, the process is rarely a comfortable one.

Although few people enjoy a job search, the guidelines in this book will point the way not only to a goal but also to a process in which the collateral benefits are educational, informative and enriching.

Seeking a job or changing jobs means embarking on a process of introspection and exploration. You need to define priorities and goals as well as research opportunities to learn "what's out there." Done properly, such a search gives you an opportunity to study market conditions, take the temperature of firms, and learn more about what's current. It also gives you the chance to interview, allowing entree to the inside of firms not otherwise accessible. How many times do you get a chance to visit competitive companies? Often you only know them by reputation, grapevine gossip or by seeing work published. And then add to your list the companies referred to you through your networking activities which you never considered. This affords a more objective view of one's worth in the marketplace as well as an evaluation of the marketplace itself.

The ability to go "inside" is all too rare. It affords a very special kind of education to those who are observant. You can learn a lot about the company image as manifested in the ambiance of the work environment. By just observing the art on the walls, the clothing people wear, their manner of speech and how you are treated, a comfort level may or may not be established. All this tells you more than any written company profile or job description and ultimately presents the opportu-

**Starting
The Search**

**Observing
Work
Environments**

nity for eye-to-eye contact, which is the best gage of all. We will, as often as time permits, visit a client to observe the work environment for all these reasons. Often the tie a man wears, the accessories worn by a woman, their method of communication, the noise level, the existence or lack of interruptions, and the attitude of the receptionist — all send very important messages. These messages are the most telling. They establish the "culture" of the firm and establish the intuitive feelings which overcome the initial objective view of a company, making your opinion subjective and attitudinal.

Many times the people I interview request I refer them on as many interviews as possible. This request stems from a sophisticated knowledge of the benefits of interviews. These people are not seeking an easy way out of the job search process. They are not less concerned about the time or effort in interviewing, nor are they concerned about exposing themselves to rejection. They want the experience and recognize the advantage of exposure. Unfortunately, I can't send people to my clients without excellent reasons, for that is just what my clients seek our services for — to save them money and the time of unnecessary interviews. However, there are other methods, as we will see, to get an inside peek at the inner workings of companies.

Learning Through Exposure

It should be obvious now why a job hunt can be a learning process. The exposure to a variety of personalities, different evaluations, feedback and critiques as well as the exposure to the atmosphere of a company can be an eye opener. It also tells you a great deal about how to make comparisons. The "corporate culture" (a overused term) is evident the minute you walk through the door. This process allows you to form opinions independently, based upon contact and not hearsay.

However, before you get through the door, there is a lot of work to be done. Above all, you want to convince people it is necessary to meet you and you want to make sure you are approaching the right people. You also want the confidence of knowing you are on the best possible trajectory, the best possible strategy for your talent and your goals. *One thing is for sure. You are going to face rejection.* It is a fact of life, so you might as well get used to it. It is a necessary part of the learning process.

Rejection in itself need only be painful if too much emotion is riding on the nature of the contact. Since it is to some degree always inevitable, it's best to recognize it as a fact of life, deal with it, and get on with the rest of your business. So don't let it stop you. You just cannot be all things to all

Coping with Rejection

people. Don't let it dim your aspirations or your determination. *Never, never take a rejection as evidence of your self-worth.* Often the ability to sustain repeated rejection is simply a matter of personal courage — and you'll definitely need a lot of courage. We all do. Too many people I know allow their fear of rejection to influence their decision-making. Sometimes it can stop them cold in their tracks. Sometimes it prevents them from trying the "impossible." Trying — always trying, taking a risk — is one of the most important characteristics for success. Measured risk- taking (not being foolhardy) is a key ingredient in the ability to move forward. So rejection or failure can be the by-product of risk. However, nothing is achieved without risk. In many ways, a certain amount of fear is a healthy self-regulating emotion—it keeps you on edge and prevents you from becoming "cocky" or, worse, arrogant. Therefore, it's necessary to take a deep breath and "go for it." And, most importantly, keep moving on. Never let setbacks or failures cloud your sight on your goals. I used to work for a firm that had a little neon sign that said "moving right along." I greatly appreciated that message glowing at me in vivid color on days that were black for me. Maybe we all need something like that to keep us moving. However, move you must—or you'll be stopped.

Who Are You? When presenting yourself to anybody, in a social or business context, the introduction process sends many messages. When embarking on a job search, you need to determine where you want to go and how to introduce yourself into a defined milieu. In order to do that successfully, you must first ask some self-searching questions.

- What am I best at?

- Is what I'm best at what I think I want to do?

- Am I sure about what kind of work I want to do?

- Where do I want to do it?

- Who do I want to do it for?

- What kind of position do I eventually want to hold, or do I want my own firm?

Until you can fairly deal with most of these questions, you're not in a position to accurately introduce yourself to a future employer. It is critical to know yourself and at least your short-term goals in order to make a focused presentation. With the right self-knowledge you can "package" yourself as an identifiable asset for hire. Our experience has proven that when a person is not clearly focused on their abilities and goals, the message sent to the interviewing individual is confused and the resulting outcome is, at best, indecision. Your goal in any interview or presentation is to present yourself as a clearly focused talent with distinct goals (even if you are not sure and are just testing the water).

Finding Your Creative Focus

So let us go over these key questions that will help establish personal priorities.

1. and 2. What are you best at? Is what you are best at what you think you want to do? What comes easily? Do you sometimes mistrust that which is easily attainable? Do you place too much value on projects that have been a struggle? Is it because you had to sweat over a project that you cannot give it up? I don't want to assume that laboring over a project means it doesn't have value, or has not met with success. It is just that very often we loose our objectivity when our effort becomes labored. Too often what comes easy is really because it's more natural to who we are. I remember when I was an undergraduate struggling with the classical empty canvas. I was studying with Robert Motherwell, who was a great influence. I had learned that painting was a metaphor and that the visual poetry was something for which I strived. However, while I loved painting, I had a great deal of trouble painting spontaneously. Everything was such a big decision, that I would stand in front of the canvas—seemingly forever. I painted slowly, although with skill. Ultimately I took a course in sculpture and found working in three dimensions a snap. But in my mind's eye I considered myself a painter. I didn't take the "sculpture thing" seriously. I mistrusted my natural talents because they were so inherently an extension of myself. I thought it was "healthier" to suffer the angst of creativity.

As a faculty member at Pratt Institute I found students doing the same thing. Perhaps they were intrigued with editorial design. But they really shone in packaging design. Or perhaps there was a fixation with creating logotypes but the person had a natural promotional bent and responded to copy concepts with strong imagery. I'm sure you see the parallels. Think about what it is that you really do best and trust in it — because that is where you will be successful.

Uphill battles are not much fun after a while.

3. Are you sure about what kind of work do you want to do? Does this question make you particularly nervous? Do you feel something is wrong if you are unsure of yourself and what it is you want to do? You probably feel the ideal is to be totally self-assured with a clear goal in sight and I'm sure you know people who seem to have all the answers. Your may

Seeking a Path find yourself envious of people who seem to be completely in control.   For sure, having that clear vision makes it easier. Nonetheless, the majority of both students and people beginning their careers are not sure about what they want to concentrate on. In fact, most people really want to have the most diversified experiences possible. Most designers prefer to be generalists. However, as we have discussed in our survey of graphic design, the marketing or geographical impositions on the field can make it difficult. So what does this "average" person do? This question leads to the next part of our inquiry:

4. and 5. Where do you want to do it? Who do you want to do it for? First, you have analyzed what it is that you do best. Now you must research the field. Read all the trade

Where periodicals, see the annuals, study the awards given, learn
To Work what current work is being done and learn who's doing it. Analyze what you see. What do you like? Where does your aesthetic focus seem to lead and what is a logical fit with your philosophical point of view ? What companies are on the same critical wavelength as the work you do best?

This is the basic methodology we use with candidates who approach us for work. We look for the visual connections. We try to detect the common threads of an aesthetic approach as exemplified through the presentation portfolio and try to match that to our clients. We think about what would "work" with various firms. For, in the last analysis, when people review portfolios and need to hire, they really want to see what they want to see. Meaning that while they may value and appreciate something other than the way they solve their visual problems, ultimately they will hire because they feel there is a strong relationship between what their firm does and your past experience or what they see in your portfolio. It is the rare person who will hire in order to establish a dramatically different design point of view.

Your Hit List

This is how to start creating the logical links, looking for the connections and making a "hit list" of companies you'd like to work for. Don't worry if there is some variety in the output of these firms. What is important is that you feel attracted to their output and you feel your own work is compatible. For those working in an area which is dissimilar — for example, you've got a job in a promotional agency, but you want to work on a magazine — an adjustment will have to be made within your portfolio samples. (See Chapter 10: Your Portfolio.) But, for now, know that you are now developing a strategy for your future and a methodology for dealing with those goals.

Long-Term Goals

6. What kind of position do you eventually want to hold, or do you want your own firm? This is obviously a question about your long-term goals. However, it is important for you to start thinking about the differences between short-term and long-term goals. So often the short-term becomes so all-encompassing with its pressures that anything that smacks of long-term isn't given any serious thought. Long-term goals are easily eclipsed by the reality of the daily struggle. Objectivity is lost and the subject doesn't even come up. This question is a memory jogger. You should start thinking about what you may eventually want to do and give serious consideration to the level of responsibility you are comfortable with. Not everyone should be a creative director or president of a

firm and take on the responsibility of running a company. Nor should everyone be a freelancer. Aš you take on jobs and new experiences, look for your role models. Think about what makes you happy. Think about the correlations between title, salary, work hours, and lifestyle as well as the differences between full-time employment and freelancing.

Networking and Portfolio Drop-offs

Your next step is to develop your personal "hit list" similar to the way I described. This will be your target list of companies for whom you would like to work. At this point you should have:

- A sense of what you want to do.

- Researched the firms to which you feel attracted and feel compatible: your "hit-list."

- In other words, you have set priorities and goals. You have your portfolio ready to go (see Chapter 10). You are ready.

The first step is to augment your list through personal contacts. If you are a student or a recent graduate, show it to your faculty. Find out who they may know at these firms and if there are other similar firms they might recommend. Go to your placement office and talk it over with a counselor. Think back to summer employment or internship contacts whom you could approach. If you are working, it is time to pull out every business card you have collected to analyze where these people are now and who might be a valuable and interesting contact. If you know people who are printers, paper sales people or other trades contacts you feel are trustworthy, ask them what they know about hiring opportunities. These service tradespeople are favorite industry couriers of all kinds of information as they travel from firm to firm. They are often asked for referrals by companies who want to hire. They represent a great way to "get the word out."

Portfolio Drop-offs: Start by telephoning the companies on your list. Start at the very top and work your way down. Don't be intimidated by the fame of the firm. The worst that can happen is that you'll be rejected and that is not the worst thing that can happen. We have discussed the relative unimportance of that act. However, who knows, you may be surprised! Ask for the art department or ask who reviews portfolios. Most importantly, you want it to be seen by the right person. Therefore, ask your questions carefully. Find out what their policy is for portfolio review. Most firms will have some kind of structure regarding reviews. It might be on a particular day of the week, or it might be only between certain hours. Ask how long you need to leave your book. And before you pick it up, make sure it's been seen! Too often someone may be called out of town or just be busy and not able to see your book. For entry level positions or for people who are not concerned about protecting their confidentiality, the portfolio drop-off is probably the quickest route to get your work seen.

While many people object to the drop-off system as being too impersonal, it has become almost an industry standard, a necessary evil. It is the most direct, time-saving way for a busy, often overworked manager to find the people he or she wants to interview in the first place. You need to remember that while your personality, motivation and goals are every bit as important as your talent, without the talent the rest isn't necessary. And when someone interviews you, to be even moderately polite, the interview must take at least a half an hour. However, it probably takes no more than two minutes at best (and probably much less) to know if a portfolio is

**Getting Your
Portfolio Seen**

interesting. That is a difficult fact for most people to accept, but it's true. The pressure this puts on you to create the best possible portfolio is enormous and we will discuss that in the next chapter. Suffice it to say that the prevalent system caters to our workaholic world, and allows the person who doesn't have a moment to spare the ability to look through portfolios in a flexible period of time, perhaps stolen moments between meetings, and determine whether a book belongs to someone they would want to meet. It is also important for young people to know that this system exists for the very experienced, too. In my firm, on a daily basis, we have to send portfolios first, even when we are submitting people for highly-paid positions. I don't want you to think that all job applications are necessarily handled this way. However, the vast majority are.

Developing Contacts

When someone has seen your work, and hopefully liked it, they will have some method of letting you know. It may be personally, through an assistant or perhaps a note. What they usually will not tell you is that they didn't like your book. People are always asking for feedback—but they rarely get it—for few want to take the time for a constructive review. The answer most often is a simple "no interest" or "not a fit." Any favorable response should, therefore, be viewed as an opportunity to create a larger network. If they were positive but didn't have an opening, could they possibly recommend other people or firms to you? Most people are really happy to try and help someone, and one contact may bring you several others. And so it goes on. A domino effect. The true meaning of networking. Don't be timid about asking secretaries, administrative assistants, creative directors, anybody who could help and seems friendly. Don't be shy and feel guilty, as if you are "using" someone. While there are negative implications to people who are indeed "users," these methods are just basic, good business practices.

Diaries for Business Contacts and Taxes

A diary or log of your activities is a necessity at this time. You should keep a record of everyone you contact, the nature of the contact, and of course the date. This information can prove to be very important as time moves on. For example, people often change jobs, and the person who indicated an interest in you and didn't have an opening may offer another kind of opportunity for you in another firm. When you are showing your portfolio over a period of many months (yes, it can take many months), it's easy to get confused as to where you've been, or perhaps who asked you to try again in two months. This information also will prove to be an important resource the next time you seek employment.

Did you know there is a tax benefit in conducting a job search? Keeping a complete record of your activities can provide tax deductions on your next return. The key is maintaining a diary or log of everything you do and everybody with whom you have contact.

The IRS is on your side when you are looking for a job within the same field of employment. This means as long as it's a graphic design or advertising position, and you don't want to do something else with your life, the costs incurred in the job search process can be a legitimate tax deduction. You must keep accurate, complete records of all your costs applicable to your search. Any directly connected expenses to your work and search including transportation, lunches, faxes, printing of resumes, even special clothing needed for an interview and any supplies (thinking of buying a computer?) must be tracked for tax purposes. Besides keeping your diary of portfolio drop-offs and interviews, keep all your receipts by either attaching them to the appropriate diary pages or start a chronological receipt file, separating your costs into travel and entertainment in one category and supplies in another. All costs that exceed 2% of your last annual gross earnings can be deducted from the next year's tax return.

Headhunters

Developing a personal affiliation with an excellent headhunter can result in one of the most important and enduring business relationships of your career. And it's free! It is the recruiter's client (the firm that wants to hire) who pays the recruiter's fee. Our firm only asks the candidate for undying loyalty (and sometimes a thank you) as recognition of our contributions to his or her future. Of course this is the moment when I should proudly proclaim the unquestionably high ethical standards of our work as well as the caliber and quality of my firm. However, putting the self-serving part of it aside, the quality and nature of the relationships we have developed over a period of many years has had a profound affect on many people's lives.

Your headhunter can become your confidant, your career counselor. You can be introduced to opportunities you would never be able to access on your own. When we have been most successful, we have met people who we have believed in, who have had a talent we could focus on and therefore introduce to a sector of our client base. We have been able to not only find them a job but track their career over many years and, in some cases, place them in several positions throughout their careers. In other words, we were fundamentally proactive in molding and guiding their careers, finding jobs, business opportunities and ultimately partnerships, acquisitions, and mergers. These people recognize the value of our relationship, often coming to us for ad hoc career advice or for advice in helping them structure job descriptions and salary/compensation packages with their firms.

The first duty of the professional executive recruiter is to service its client, the firm who wishes to hire, who has asked the recruiter for help to solve a hiring need and who pays the recruiter's fee. The recruiter can only properly refer candidates to the client when the recruiter fully understands the personality, capabilities and professional goals of the candidate. So the recruiter walks a fine line between servicing the clients in the best way possible and helping the candidate almost as a "rep," or artist's representative. That is why, so often, our candidates become our clients. And, since we are always on the lookout for new talents, the recruiter can also become a networking resource for the entry-level candidate. However, it should also be remembered what a recruiter cannot do. A recruiter cannot be your only source, for no one has access to every possibility. And a recruiter cannot be successful for everybody, so recruitment firms may not be able to solve your immediate problems. They may, however, turn out to be an excellent resource the next time around. The best advice is to try to get access to more than one recruiter and see how the relationship develops. The quality of communication between the two of you will determine the quality of your future association.

A Simple "Thank You"

It's a simple maxim: The more successful your networking strategy is, the more expanded your contact list will become. The sheer number of diverse people you'll meet will be an education in itself. You are utilizing many resources: faculty, mentors, friends, business associates, trades people, and executive recruiters (headhunters). And those resources are recommending other contacts. Along the way many people will show an interest in your future and take time from their busy day to avail you of their expertise. It's time then to say a formal thank you with a simple note, and show you not only have good manners but a good business sense. It has often been the finishing cap to an interview for a highly competitive position! I often tell students who have spent a great deal of time and money on their education that the best business move can be achieved for the cost of a stamp. As previously noted, people move around a lot in this business and you never know when you'll meet up with someone again. The platitude, "it's a very round world" is amazingly true! So remember your manners and say "thank you".

Resumes

There is an infinite number of methods to produce a satisfying resume, and many firms offer professional resume writing services. I do not recommend resume services for creative people. My experience has proven that the resume which accompanies a portfolio has special requirements. Most often this resume is not viewed by itself, but serves as an companion to a visual presentation. However, when submitted by itself, it must still be able to stand alone, if only as an introduction to the portfolio and/or interview which follows.

The resume that accompanies a portfolio has to have the following characteristics: It must be clear, concise, clean (no folded corners, creases, or smudges) and without errors. Resumes do not have to be professionally printed, and I am ambivalent about using a resume to make an unusual design statement. The bottom line is when the design works well, it's great. However, I have seen too many over-designed resumes create a negative impact. Your safest bet is a simple, clearly laid out (that's design), highly legible resume. Currently most resumes are type set on computer. A typewritten resume is still acceptable but has become a rarity.

The computer has made the possibility of multiple resumes a flexible and easy option. Having more than one resume is often an excellent idea. One of the most applicable uses would be to change the "objectives" when necessary. It is an appropriate choice for the person who can have different directions to pursue. Just as you can manipulate the structure of your portfolio (See Chapter 10: Your Portfolio) you can have two resumes with two separate objectives. For example, you might like to alternately stress your management experience or your creative experience. This could be accomplished by the manner in which your current job responsibilities are emphasized, by focusing on one more than the other.

Some "do not's" regarding paper choice: Do not use dark-colored paper. It cannot be photocopied. Paper that is too heavy cannot be faxed. For the sake of good taste, do not use pastels that are best left for cosmetic packaging. Some people choose to have their resume on two kinds of paper, one for reproduction and one as a statement of taste values. Paper choices are an important part of the designer's toolbox, so naturally the selection for a resume is a statement in itself.

Be sure that whatever format you use, your layout is clean, logical, and easy to read. Lastly, remember, to write succinctly, with clarity. Make sure your resume honestly represents your experience without misrepresenting, and be careful neither to omit nor exaggerate important responsibilities. Always, always proofread for typos and spelling. Have someone else proof for you as well. Two or three pairs of eyes are best. It can be a killer factor on an otherwise terrific resume (and can loose you an opportunity).

The following is a sample resume that offers one of many possible solutions. It is clearly meant as a suggested format for a resume to accompany a portfolio. It will, nonetheless, have enough information to "stand alone," or work independently, if submitted by itself. The format is set up to give you instructions within the form of a sample resume. It is, with a few exceptions, the form we give to applicants in my office when we feel it is needed.

Sample Resume

(Two pages at most with your last name in the upper right corner of the second page and "Page 2" added and, no pictures, please!)

Name
Address
City, State, Zip Code
Home phone number
Work (or message) phone number

OBJECTIVE

Only if goals are very specific. Two sentences at most. Consider two resumes, one with and one without objectives. Consider multiple resumes with different objectives.

EXPERIENCE

List your last position first (see example below). If you are currently employed, show date as "to present." Job title must be included. Describe the level of your responsibilities (what you really do). Include a client list (who you do it for). The longer you have worked, the less you need to list experiences from more than six to eight years ago. Assume you will get your next position based on your experiences from the last five to eight years. For positions that are before that point, only list the name of firm, your title and perhaps a few clients at most. Be sure to include in your recent work experience description: the title of the person to whom you reported, the quality and level of client contact (middle management, upper management), budgetary or fiscal responsibility, supervision of vendors, support staff freelancers, art direction of illustration and/or photography, and interfacing with copywriters or marketing, any hands-on or direction of computer functions, knowledge of production, and any other applicable points that show responsibility and accountability.

Sample
1990 -Present   **AMERICAN CORPORATION:**
                       Art Director/Designer

                       Responsibilities include design concepts, execution
                       and presentation of design comprehensives, manage-
                       ment and supervision of staff of three, freelancers,
                       desktop publishing and computer production staff,
                       selection and art direction of photographers and
                       illustrators, client contact, budget estimates and
                       proposals, and on-press supervision. Projects include
                       all required corporate communications, including
                       company magazines, quarterly reports, press kits and
                       newsletters.

ENTRY LEVEL   List all work experience using the same principles as
APPLICANTS   above. Be sure to list first any career-related experi-
                       ences, such as internships, summer work, and work-
                       shops. Stress experiences that included interpersonal
                       skills (selling, working as a waiter, etc.) or those that
                       required problem-solving, computers or detail inten-
                       sive work.

EDUCATION   College and postgraduate work only. Omit high
                       school. Include special classes or training pro-
                       grams. Be sure to include date of graduation,
                       degree and major.

                       Sample:
                       Pratt Institute: B.F.A., Graphic Design; 1992

SPECIAL SKILLS   Very important for junior and mid-level positions that
                       rely on a high degree of technical expertise. Computer
                       knowledge and software programs must be included.

SPECIAL INTERESTS	Include only if applicable to your job search. Omit hobbies, such as traveling and gourmet cooking. (Everybody is and does.) However, if you are applying for a position on a magazine stressing travel or skiing, your personal interests are important.
PERSONAL	It is preferable to omit personal details unless you want a relocation, at which point marital status and children can become a factor. Birth dates are optional because there are legal restrictions on requesting this information (as well as age, race, and religion) in an interview or application.
AWARDS & PROFESSIONAL RECOGNITION	Always a plus to include if they are recognized industry awards pertinent to your professional life. However, do not include the actual awards in your portfolio. For example, include awards from higher educational institutions, professional design or advertising organizations, and omit a award for painting in a local show.
REFERENCES	Always state: "Furnished or available upon request."
SALARY REQUIREMENTS	Never indicate a salary history or a salary requirement on a resume. This information can be included in a cover letter, if necessary.

As always, when dealing with resumes or interviews or life in general, what can go wrong will go wrong. I thought it would be amusing, and possibly educational, to tell you of some resumes that would have been better left in a drawer. We collect them under a file called "Resumes I have known but not forgotten."

- Under Skills: "I can do the Rubic's Cube in 60 seconds."

- The Asian designer who, under Foreign Languages, listed "English."

- The recent graduate's resume took four pages.

- Special Skills: "Left Handed"

- Under Organizations: The National Association of Floor Covering Women

- The award for the best closing statement on a covering letter: " I am 60 years of age. My Mom is ninety-three, and feeling fine. Dad died of WWI wounds 57 years after having been gassed and shot. My health is excellent and my energy and enthusiasm beyond average."

- Resumes which have a picture covering a least 1/4 of the page.

- The person who had a sex change operation and noted: "born August 23, 1949 — born again June 12, 1984."

- The proofreader who wrote "...support teamwork ethic, illicting enthusiastic participation..."! This same person went on to say, "Hired two new proofers to replace one unreliable one." (Some proofreading, and what a budget!)

And under the file, "Illiteracies We Have Known" is the person who went to Fairleigh Dickinson University and spelled it "Fairlegh" on our application.

Choosing a Job

Now your job search is becoming effective and you have received an offer from a firm. Once you have gotten over the immediate rush of excitement at a job offer, you need to ask yourself if this position is really the one you want. This is not necessarily an easy question. You will have to consider many conflicting issues. How much do you need to work (it's called paying the rent)? How much do you want to keep your other options open? How much do you like or trust your future employer? But the most important question should be: *Do you want the work produced by that company in your portfolio?* While we'll discuss career building in greater detail in Chapter 11: it is important for you to consider some of these issues now, for they cross-reference. The overriding issue should be the knowledge that the quality of work in your portfolio will always determine your next job. It's a simple as that! Therefore, you must always consider the work you see in the portfolio of a possible employer will be the quality of work entering your portfolio once you work for them. It's not that you won't have some creative freedom, or contribute your talents. It's what the firm's client base is and requires, what the firm's reputation is based on, and how they attract new clients. It is a rare time that you can expect to work on projects which are significantly different than the firm's previous work.

Non-Creative Positions

These areas offer wonderful and important opportunities for the designer who learns their business, managerial or technical acumen is superior to their creative capabilities. It is not uncommon for individuals to experience a reassessment of their skills after a few years in the field. The person who is attracted to account services is the individual who enjoys problem solving and contact with clients more than the actual hands-on process of design. Business development is a highly compensated area for the entrepreneur who can successfully market a sales effort for creative services. Studio managers operate from a knowledge base of production methods and strong organizational skills. All these directions provide key positions in firms with significantly less competition in the hiring process than creative positions. Employers perceive these areas and skills as invaluable components in their organizations and the person who enters these positions with a creative background adds the substantial element of design sensitivity to the position's qualifications. Let's look at them separately.

Studio Managers / Production Managers

These positions represent a valued component in the design office for it is these individuals who often represent the "glue" that connects the design processes and makes everything happen. These managers must have a strong sense of design, computer technology, printing, and materials. They must have excellent organization skills and be generally detail orientated. Their management of internal personnel, outside vendors, purchasing, budgets and scheduling makes them ultimately the point-person to insure a project is delivered on time and on budget. Excellent people skills and an equal capacity for verbal and written communication are a must. A firm's profit or loss status can hinge on the skills of the studio or production manager. Salary compensation packages for studio and production managers are usually equivalent to middle management design positions, but this does not mean they cannot rise above that level. Some of these managers eventually become partners in design firms.

Account Services/ Account Executives

While these positions are discussed in some detail in Chapter 3: The Identity Business, account services personnel function in most other areas of the design field as well. *These are the individuals who hone their strategic skills beyond their creative ones.* For the designer making a career segue, they will find this an important niche in design, for the account team is an integral part of the creative process. Account services offers the opportunity to work with the client in the initial stages of project development, setting the strategy and criteria. It is an intellectually stimulating period in the scope of the project. The account people are often responsible for translating these criteria to the creative staff and all the follow-up liaison work between client and creative. They usually have project responsibility for writing proposals and monitoring budgets. While these positions are not necessarily filled by people with a creative education, they do offer opportunities to designers looking for a career change. Account service managers, account executives or project managers are middle management or senior management positions and therefore their compensation falls within those ranges. (See Survey, p.188.)

By the nature of their positions, account people are exposed to the new business development process as practiced by different design consultancies. They are sometimes brought into that process, asked to assist new business efforts or perhaps to expand business by developing additional components to existing projects. Thus they enter the sales arena.

New Business Development/ Marketing

For some the sales process is totally intimidating. For others it is perceived without fear of rejection and almost as a sport. The ability to successfully market a creative service is the most important component to any design business. Bringing in the business is, of course, critical to any firm's survival. In the past most new clients came to design offices through the referral process. Firms existed (and still do) by reputation. The past years have seen an expansion of the aggressive marketing of design services. Most firms no longer simply rely on the referral process or on the sole ability of the principals to develop business. To many, aggressive marketing can include any combination of researchers, telemarketing, account services personnel, and marketing executives solely devoted to the new business effort. Some of these marketing executives enter design with an MBA degree. They may have had prior experience as a product manager in a corporation or worked in an advertising agency on an account team. However, many of these executives started their careers in design and found they had a knack for the business side. Some moved into this area as designers who became account services executives. Some designers went on to get their MBA's. Since it is apparent how critical these individuals are to a firm's success, it should be no surprise to know that their compensation would be tied to their effectiveness. They are usually paid a salary plus performance-based incentives, most often in the form of commissions. This career track can easily result in an equity position or firm partnership.

Freelancing

What do you do if you don't have too many other options and need to work? Try to consider working on a freelance basis instead of on a staff. The down side is that you won't get health and vacation benefits, but you will be able to continue looking for a better job. What if the employer doesn't want a freelance arrangement? Take the job — but try not to stay too long. Most likely you shouldn't stay more than six months to a year. You'll probably get some good studio experience and be a little more seasoned for the next job search.

Freelancing is an excellent way of sampling a variety of work environments. Although you'll be paid more on an hourly basis than you would on staff, you won't receive benefits, you won't have economic security and the number of hours you work will be irregular. As it is impossible to live without medical coverage in today's society, be sure you are covered, either by yourself or through a family member. Many people like to freelance because of the sheer diversity of experience in the work environment, the flexible hours and

Tax Benefits

the tax benefits they receive from the IRS as an "independent." This is a good time to get some expert advice from an accountant who can instruct you on the proper forms of record-keeping. When you are freelancing, you are self-employed and therefore entitled to the business expenses attached with being self-employed. It can be an excellent way of life for the more independent soul. It also means going without the security of a full-time position and not feeling a part of a team. Freelancing on a temporary basis serves well for the person who is holding out for the "perfect" job or for the person who wants a break from moving from one permanent position to another. It also represents an excellent

The "Foot in the Door"

solution to bad economic periods. When jobs are scarce, there is always an increase of freelance opportunities. Freelancing can serve an additional purpose when it allows both company and employee to get used to each other. Some possibilities are the trial testing period before a full-time offer is extended or the proverbial "foot in the door" opportunity at a highly desirable firm. From the employer's viewpoint it's often used as a method of "try before you buy."

A negative aspect to freelancing, however, is the consideration that the process rarely contributes anything substantial to a person's portfolio. Most often you will be asked to work on the implementation of assignments, instead of seeing them

Will Your Portfolio Benefit?

from beginning to end. There is hardly an opportunity to put work into your portfolio that shows any real personal contribution or impact. If you freelance for too long (more than a year or 18 months) the results could be damaging to your portfolio. After a time your work would become dated and you could have difficulty showing what you did for that period of time. There are, of course, people who are permanent freelancers. In this instance we need to make distinctions between freelancing and being self-employed. The subtle nuance is the assumption that after a prolonged period the individual is really self-employed (although there may be no other employees working for the individual) and truly committed to independent status. If, for economic or other reasons, work dries up and the designer wants a staff position,

Are You Self-Employed?

we have great difficulty placing people. While the foremost reason maybe the structure of their portfolio, there is always a latent suspicion in the employer's mind that the candidate will return to a freelance or independent status as soon as it's viable. This is a realistic acknowledgment of the different goals of independent designers who are very content with the lifestyle and income afforded through their freelance business. Certainly it is an option to consider as one of the many paths available.

Your Portfolio

10 Your portfolio is your most important expression of everything you are and want to be. It is a unique display of your talent and an exhibit of your experience. While it is a visual expression, it demonstrates a psychological shorthand that must tell your special story. And since life experiences or personal histories are never alike, it follows that no two portfolios are alike. How individual the portfolios are is a constant fascination to all those who are in a position to review many "books" (in the jargon of our business). They are analogous to human faces who have some similar characteristics, but are never actually the same. The structure of portfolios must always be flexible, always subject to the needs of the individual, but should express in the best possible way what you have done, what you can do and what you want to do. *It is therefore the visual embodiment of your past, present and future.*

Accepting this portentous pronouncement, is it any wonder that the content and presentation of a portfolio is, without question, the single most anxiety-producing element and the most critical part in the entire job search process? While I have gone to great lengths to show how important every other element of your persona is, and that your ability to be successful is not totally dependent upon your visual talent, it is nonetheless your portfolio that makes it all possible. It will get you in the door, after which your other skills must take charge. Remember, in the vast majority of application processes, your work will precede your persona as an introduction. Often you will drop off your portfolio or send transparencies of your work (see Chapter 9, Getting Started). Without the talent and its proper presentation the rest is simply not possible. And to compound the pressure placed on this "simple" book, the number of people who loose opportu-

Impact and Content

nities not due to their talent but because of the condition of their portfolio is simply astonishing. It is not only astonishing but sometimes cruel, for without a knowledgeable person pointing the way, many get lost. We have seen many people hired because we insisted on an interview after the portfolio had been rejected. We accomplish this difficult task only because of the level of confidence we command as recruiters. Lack of information or misinformation can eliminate years of valuable study and training. Obviously, this chapter will not only point the way, but give you some important insights into how people evaluate the look of portfolios when they need to hire.

Format

Many people like to be rather dogmatic about the construction of a portfolio. Examples would include dictums as to how one should only use boards or perhaps certain kinds of folios. Others advise that your portfolio should stand out from the crowded masses of black books and make a statement! They advise that you should construct a unique personalized statement. While we have reviewed many unique, wonderful books, our experience has shown that attempts at these unusual constructions have proven to be a disaster in most cases. A trip to any fully-stocked art supply store will quickly confirm the selection available is so large, that the number of choices and the decision of what to select is difficult enough. The critical decisions regarding your portfolio format should relate to content and ability to avail you with a flexible system. You need to analyze the essence of your work. Is it primarily two- or three-dimensional? Is the two-dimensional work flat or does it include pamphlets and brochures? Would the three-dimensional work be best served through photography? Maybe there will be times that you need a combination of formats to adequately show phases of a project. You need to approach your portfolio with an attitude of what is logical for the specific problem and not feel locked into a format. There are no rules as to right or wrong. The only rule is what "works" makes for success. And you must give clear consideration to size.

Size

Somehow the size factor is often the last to be considered. However, size also affects weight. Therefore you should think about how you will feel carrying your book, looking for work for perhaps days, weeks, or months? How will it hold up on buses, trains, subways and planes? Since the use of a messenger service may sometimes be necessary, would you want the service to refuse to carry it because it's too heavy? Would you want to see your portfolio have to be checked in at an airport? Will it fit into an overhead compartment on a plane? Would you ever have to ship your portfolio? In that case, size will affect cost.

Will you want two portfolios? Often it helps to have either a duplicate or books that serve different purposes. Duplicate portfolios can have a variety of purposes, not the least being the safety factor of not ever losing everything that is the key to your future. You should protect yourself by documenting your work through photography. We have seen several examples of books being lost, and the results are heartbreaking. One recent graduate lost her portfolio in a subway. She simply forgot to take it with her when she got off the train. Portfolios have been lost through moving, accidents, and fire. Don't let it ever happen to you. I must add that only once in over 10 years did we ever have a client lose a book. It happened at a large advertising agency. Most firms, ours included, have tightly controlled systems for logging books in and out. While you must protect yourself from accidents, do not let the fear of losing your portfolio prevent you from dropping your work off to be seen. Occasionally we encounter someone who refuses to leave their book, insisting on an interview. The net result of that attitude is to be cut off from opportunities.

For some reason students seem to have the largest portfolios. In contrast there seems to be a equation that *the more experienced the designer, the smaller the book*. One graphic designer has his portfolio on a series of small formica-like chips held together by a key chain. Another person reduced his presentation to a 4 x 5 box of transparencies, presented like a deck of cards. While these examples demonstrate an individualization of presentation and a move away from the "black book" standard, I mention them because their realized objective was to condense as well as personalize. The message is, size bears no relation to content. Size also seems to bear no relation to the person carrying it. We often are amazed to see the smallest individuals bringing in books that we can't lift!

Choosing a Format

So, what works? Boards are heavy. Acetate scratches. Transparencies can be expensive. And what about a group of samples that greatly vary in size? While there are no absolute answers the following are some suggestions based on current modes. When deciding on size consider the average of most of your pieces and work within that framework. Oversized pieces such as posters should be reduced by utilizing 4 x 5 transparencies.

When having your work photographed, get it done as professionally as possible. If you are in school, seek out in-school photo services or photography majors. Most working designers know someone who can do them a favor. Obviously the quality of the photography means everything. It is awkward to have to apologize for poorly photographed work during an interview. It also sends a negative message.

Transparencies work nicely when mounted in black board frames. Three-dimensional work; packaging, exhibition, and industrial design should all be photographed. You can combine 35mm slides and 4 x 5 transparencies — sometimes even on the same mounting board, if it makes sense. And you should combine photographed work with the actual pieces or sketches when appropriate. At least a sampling of actual printed material should always be included, for people want to touch, smell, and feel the finished product. Slides most often lose much of the impact of the typography as well as any sense of the paper and quality of printing. However, slides do have the advantage of hiding the rough edges on hand work. Anything drawn or cut and pasted always looks better when photographed and reduced. Remembering to periodically document your work — through slides, finished and rough art — as a safety measure against loss is advice worth repeating.

Sketches

A few words about the underrated and integral value of sketch books, roughs, and comps. They should definitely be included in the back of your book. Many people cringe when asked to include what are often messy sketches. Don't worry. They should be placed in a neat folder and labeled appropriately. They are a key ingredient in your presentation, for they indicate the process of your thoughts, your act of problem-solving, the variety of scope of your thinking, and often exhibit a preferable realization of a solution than the finished product shown in your book (if they have been killed by a client or proven too impractical). Your sketches show the breadth of your imagination. They are the key to the essence of your fundamental creative personality. No person that I truly respect would view a book and not expect to see these drawings.

Finished Art

Flat print work such as editorial, identity programs, packaging design, and labels are most often displayed in a spiral or bound acetate book in which the pages can be moved or replaced. The quality of acetate has improved and scratching is not as much of a problem as in the past, but it still exists. No one has yet seemed to develop ring binders which close so tightly that they will not catch the pages as you turn them. Just remember, no matter what format you choose, your presentation should be immaculate. If necessary, you must replace the acetate as needed. Never show anything that's dirty or dog-eared. When including a sample that has multiple pages, such as a brochure or annual report, freestanding acetate sleeves both protect your work and make the entire project accessible to the viewer. If you want to include a publication in which you were responsible for only certain pages, tabbing or clipping the work becomes an acceptable method. Since you will most likely be asked to drop off your portfolio, you may want to include a written description, index of the portfolio's contents or labels on certain items if it makes sense. Remember, though, the resume accompanying your work will indicate your level of responsibility.

Presentation

Everything you include in your book says something to the viewer about your personality, talent and attitudes toward work. How you treat your work, tells the viewer not only how you respect your own work but how you will respect your future employer's projects. Needless to say, your presentation must be of the highest caliber. It sounds obvious and simple, but you can't imagine how many portfolios we see that do not fulfill these requirements. Some people literally throw work into a portfolio and just zip it up. Whatever format you choose for presentation, it has to be clean, logical, and flexible in order to reflect your interests. As to its flexibility and order of presentation, you must consider everything discussed in this passage along with the suggestions made in Chapter 9, Getting Started, for the two are completely interrelated. One relates to the inner self, the other to the outward manifestation of that self. In order to tailor your presentation to the firms you approach, you need the physical capability to communicate the inner reality.

Why Order is Critical

I always suggest that the first project exposed to the viewer when they open your portfolio is your best. It is your initial introduction. You really do have only a few important seconds to create a first impression. Your "hello," appearance and handshake set the tone for all that follows. So too does the first piece in your portfolio. The tone should be one of excitement and anticipation for all that is to follow. It sets the stage. It dictates the psychological atmosphere that will predispose the viewer's thinking to your other work. This is the very important psychological "short-hand" mentioned in the first paragraph of this chapter. You must create an anticipation that your book is going to be a wonderful experience for the viewer. After that, you must follow with the most appropriate work for the particular situation and end with a piece almost as good as the piece with which you started.

How Many Samples?

Everyone always wants to know how many pieces to include in a portfolio. As usual there are no magic formulas, but a portfolio shouldn't have fewer than 10 to 12 samples of projects and probably no more than 15 to 18. If you have 20, you probably have gone too far. This is clearly a case of quality and not quantity. The old adage that *your portfolio is as strong as the weakest piece* in it is absolutely true! It is amazing how often a person is refused an interview because one or two pieces were included that should have been left in the drawer. Try to include as many projects as possible that show implementation of an idea or a campaign. The implementation of a project should be considered as part of the whole project and therefore not as additional samples in your book. Ideas that show many components and applications are better that a single solution with a single purpose. Consistency is a tremendous characteristic of a well-composed book. *Inconsistency is perceived as lack of taste or lack of focus.* Both characteristics are frowned upon and have a negative effect. The concept of consistency in showing a body of creative work is a subjective and abstract process. Any critique of work is by its nature totally subjective. However, developing consistency in the level or quality of the work is a separate issue from consistency in the type of projects shown.

Consistency and Style

We are all familiar with the question of style. Most well-known fine artists or graphic design icons of this century have a style that is easily recognized. We can spot a Rauchenberg or Warhol in a minute. We all know Paul Rand's work. But could we recognize all the stylistic changes in Milton Glaser's work over the years? It is a question of consistency of approach versus a personal style.

The strongest portfolios show a consistency of approach toward design. But we need to consider what to show a prospective employer. The book also needs to address specific business directions. Therefore the difficult balance must include a consistency of projects specific to a business direction. To this end, how does your book address the prospective firm's business focus? What do they do and how do they do it? Therefore what do you show? I have always believed in the philosophy that people want to see what they want to see. So I recommend establishing a consistency of business direction in the portfolio. It is the reality of the marketplace that creates these demands. We discussed why one needs a flexible format. This is the optimum moment to utilize that flexibility. Some of our tricks of the trade are to often rearrange work, delete or add if the missing links are available to produce a whole response which:

- reflects your individual goals

- reflects your level of talent and experience

- functions logically to the needs of the marketplace.

When we hear of a job opening, will ask a person whether they are interested in submitting their work. We will describe the position in detail. If the designer wants to be considered as a candidate, we may, if we think it's necessary, ask them to show X, Y, and Z; delete S and T; and ask if they perhaps have some samples of R that would be appropriate in relation to the job. However, as a general modus operandi, we will not show any work if we feel it's not up to the client's standards.

Since a "tight" and objective sampling of your own work is extremely difficult to achieve, try to get private criticism from as many people as possible by showing your book to those whom you respect. While it is unlikely that they will all agree, you should get a general consensus to consider. Ultimately, it must be your decision as to what to include. However, beware of emotionally attaching yourself to projects that were very difficult or involved a great deal of work. They are hard to let go and exclude, but they may not be the best representation of your work. It's a similar syndrome to in the decision-making process of choosing a field of endeavor. (See Chapter 9, Who Are You?) At the same time, you should always have the confidence to stick to those beliefs in which you have a strong conviction.

Changing Work Goals

Often a person wants to diversify their experiences and to change their goals or field of specialty. This is a wonderful way of staying fresh. An example would be a person who has spent several years working on magazines and decides he or she "wants out" of editorial design. The challenge presented by this type of shift is a portfolio which has become very specialized. As stated, most often people want to see what they want to see. This means that if they are seeking a packaging designer, they want to see packaging. For a designer to merely express an "interest" in working in that field is simply not enough to demonstrate the ability, nor will a passing knowledge or a few packaging projects do the trick. The only way I have seen a career segue possible is when:

- The designer makes a strong attempt to find freelance work in the area of choice and then include it in the book.

- The designer reworks existing projects into another format or includes "spec" work demonstrating his or her ability in the area of choice.

- There exists some logical connection within the essential character of the work. Examples would include utilizing the art direction of fashion photography toward another direction or perhaps an editorial designer moving into annual reports.

- Personal persuasion: A person is somehow able to convince another to give the designer a chance.

In any case, the common denominator is to put "other" work into your book that will clearly demonstrate your flexibility as a designer. It is difficult and takes enormous effort to develop "new" work or samples, especially when you have a full-time job. However, it is a way to make change possible for you.

Although I often make these recommendations, few people have the energy follow them. Some years ago, however, I suggested this approach to an editorial designer who wanted to be considered for a position at a sales promotional agency. I knew they'd never seriously consider someone from, in this case, a computer magazine. The designer took my advice and reworked with some of his editorial spreads by cutting and pasting them into promotion pieces. He did a splendid job and was hired.

Shared Projects and Work Ethics

The content guidelines outlined here obviously apply to samples from either work experience or from school projects. In any discussion of portfolio content, the question of shared projects or projects that have had a strong collaborative input must be addressed. As a young designer you may find yourself working on a project in which the concept or art direction has been set. You may be asked to do the type specifications, crop photos, work within an established grid or pagination, and so forth. Yet that contribution is important and the work deserves to be included. Ethically, your resume should indicate the level of your responsibility and in an interview you should indicate what your role was on a given project.

Duplicate Samples

Our clients sometimes complain about "duplicate" portfolios. Perhaps they are seeing more than one person from the same firm. This becomes a sticky wicket when the individuals work on the same level and there is no clear reporting structure. An example would be two or three art directors leaving a firm who worked for the same client. If the same projects appear in each portfolio, it's natural to raise questions of conflict. As long as you clearly represent your role in a project there shouldn't be any inquiries requiring you to validate your contribution. When you don't clearly represent your role, the fallout can be quite destructive. Any misrepresentation weakens everyone's position. The worst condemnation is the phrase "I don't think the work is his." The word "think" casts a long shadow. Once you are questioned, it is hard to get into the clear light again.

This subject is appropriate, on a more complicated level, to senior-level staff leaving a firm to start their own business.

The Ethics of Assigning Credit

Their ability to present their past work is key to establishing their credentials to new clients. It is within the same guidelines and principles for any designer to have the freedom to demonstrate experience and creativity and it is general industry practice to do so as long as the work shown is accurately described. The bottom line is to be completely honest and fully describe the conditions under which any work was done, crediting the appropriate firms or individuals. If there is a dispute, legal action will often follow. (See Chapter 11, Hiring Practices.)

Today, we perceive a renewed emphasis on business ethics as having significance and value. This represents another aspect of the 1990's back-lash to the "anything method that is profitable is acceptable" attitudes of the 1980's. The designer, whose career is built on individual creativity, must always recognize the need to protect that individuality in a business world that often structures work through team efforts. The designer needs to establish a delicate balance between being a "team player" and a creative "individualist." At the end of the day, your talent and personal reputation are all you have.

In the 1990's these are both old-fashioned and new-fashioned values. Fortunately for some, they never changed. To cut corners for expediency's sake is ultimately to cut off opportunities. It's an old platitude, but true, that the world is very round. I have seen business opportunities lost because of word on the "street" about "indiscretions" made many years before. The individuals losing the opportunities are never told why and probably would never associate it with a long gone past history. The dangers of this word of mouth or innuendo is clear. Perhaps it's true, or perhaps not — but it exists.

Avoiding Negative Reputations

There is another dimension to the negative fallout of questionable business ethics. Many designers will not take a job with a firm whose reputation is in doubt. The industry "grapevine" is very powerful. Often, the telling points are how much turnover a firm may be experiencing. We have often seen examples of this attitude when designers leave jobs because of disapproval of the owner's methods of doing business. Since our subject is creatively-driven businesses, those firms are, in the last analysis, significantly hurt by a cut-off of their prime resource, creative talent.

In short, mistakes made in your twenties or thirties can follow you into your forties and fifties. Value yourself, value your reputation and others will hold the same opinion. It's not being a Pollyanna, it's good business. Ultimately, we may discuss ethics and to what degree one is "comfortable" within a given situation; but even for the most pragmatic of business people, the bottom line is the ability to maintain the "critical mass" of the business. In short, no one wants to diminish their business because of incorrect ethical decisions.

Production Work in a Creative Book

Sometimes the designer, especially in a first job, will be asked to do mundane, non-creative work. Perhaps you may have taken a job doing production on work you don't like, but the job at that time was necessary. In other words, you may have worked on projects you won't want to include as part of your portfolio, but, nonetheless, you have spent a significant time at that job. It shows on your resume and you don't want it to represent your level of creativity. The solution to this quandary is to put the work into your portfolio, but into a rear pocket or a separate folder. It should be marked "production" and may be next to another similar folder marked "sketches." It still represents a quality of experience that should positively add to the body of your work. By separating it out, it will not conflict with your creative persona.

Still Can't Make the Final Content Decisions?

When all else fails in trying to decide which samples to delete, I suggest the following: Take six or seven pieces, lay them out for comparison, and delete the weakest one. Now do the same with five or six other pieces. Shuffle the remaining samples together and repeat the process. In this manner you will constantly cut down the number of samples as you increase the quality.

Why Your Portfolio Will Never Be Finished

I'm sure you can understand the rationale behind this statement. You may not realize that some designers do consider their portfolio finished. It is a mistake to do so. Just as there are designers who can never quite deliver a completed book because they are so enthusiastic about their "latest" project just coming off press that must be included, there are those who are perfectly content to present the same book to everyone for all purposes and for a long time. Clearly it is this person who is "stuck" in time, never growing or being able to demonstrate something new.

Your portfolio should always to be considered as a work in progress representing the last five years or so of your work experiences. You should always be thinking about updating it and wrestling with the process of addition and deletion. As you grow professionally, your attitudes, point of view, and creative style will grow as well. New jobs, new interests and new perspectives will all flavor the content of your portfolio. Your portfolio is a current and demanding diary of your work

and personality. It always requires your care and attention.
And while you must keep it current, never discard the past.
Keep it filed. It will become a valuable personal history. I
hope you'll enjoy these souvenirs as much as you'll enjoy
your future.

Hiring Practices

11

Looking for work with a realistic expectation means recognizing the full scope of the dynamics at play. It means having a "big picture" viewpoint and thinking beyond your own objectives. Otherwise you will get lost in the trap of a consuming subjective experience in which your agenda seems to be the only issue. Most individuals are so wrapped up with their own priorities, they do not focus on what may be the primary need of the employer (the very person with whom they desire to develop a relationship). For that matter, many employers can only focus on their immediate dilemma of finding someone to fill a specific spot and solve their pressing problems. Rarely do they relate to how they felt when they looked for a job.

Establishing Business Relationships

The key ingredient for a successful relationship is the synergy that develops between employer and employee. The only way that can be accomplished is for the employer and prospective employee to recognize and understand each other's point of view. For the candidate looking for work, understanding the employer's needs is the first step toward creating that relationship. Often it will also spell success in the job search. The employer's recognition of the candidate's goals completes this equation.

It is my belief that the quality of these employee/employer relationships defines both of their futures. Their relationship also defines the quality of the product they produce. The quality of the end product will determine the success of the firm and the future career paths of the individuals involved. Employer and employee should recognize the essential fact that, in a creatively-driven business, *people are the inventory and they walk out the door every night*. Therefore the level of talent and commitment possessed by employee or demanded by the employer establishes the internal synergy of the rela-

**Guideposts
to Success**

tionship and the profound power one has over the other. This synergy controls the essential give and take in a creative business relationship. The possible issues of personality, office politics, ambition, work environment, sex, culture, title, money, work ownership, the quality of the work and clients, and many other more subtle elements create the dynamics of successful or unsuccessful relationships. These components are key guideposts in making decisions when questions of hiring, firing, leaving, or taking a position need to be acted on. Most people erroneously discount the role of personality and emotionalism in the decision-making process, and both employer and employee may assume that position and money are the usual motivating ingredients. The extent and variety of these issues should always be factored into your thinking and you will approach situations with a far more pragmatic and sophisticated outlook. If there is an inability for both sides to maintain this strategic business relationship, their lack of synchronization can contribute to the decline of the company.

And Failure

There are dramatic examples of how firms have been crippled by the loss of key talent who left for greener pastures. The issues at work are more often creative freedom and recognition than title and money. For example, in 1987 Lord Geller Frederico Einstein, a New York agency of major reputation, which was part of J. Walter Thompson and owned by the WPP Group, was shattered by the defection of much of their creative staff. Both partners and employees left, claiming lack of creative freedom, and formed Lord Einstein O'Neill & Partners with Young & Rubicam as the parent company. The move placed the valuable IBM contract in jeopardy. Today, after a landmark lawsuit in favor of the parent WPP Group, Lord Einstein O'Neill & Partners does not exist, the highly valued accounts have flown to other agencies, and many lives and careers have been unalterably changed and some destroyed.

In The Beginning: The creative relationship between employer and employee
The Hiring begins in the hiring process. This can be fragile, dependent on a special synergy and ending when one of the two breaks away for another goal. Both parties participate in an important pas de deux: joining together in a creative effort in which the quality of the choreography determines the success of the business as well as their careers.

The beginning is the formation of hiring policies and procedures that combine these talents into successful business partnerships (and sometimes the development of important mentor relationships). The dynamics of this subject is often discussed only behind closed doors and rarely in print. Nonetheless these difficult questions are critical to anyone developing a career:

- How do the decisions get made on both sides of the fence?

- What are the priorities and criteria that determine hiring policies and the acceptance of the employee?

- What are the underlying agendas?

- Just what is the "chemistry" of a successful interview?

Critical honesty is as rare a response as it is a painful process. Furthermore it can be a dangerous course as it can make the individual vulnerable to all sorts of retaliatory actions. Due to the subjectivity of many decisions and the general unwillingness of employers to say anything negative about an individual, the focus is shifted elsewhere during interviews or in conversation with recruiters. The true concerns don't surface and the person only experiences rejection without constructive feedback. Although this dynamic can be very subtle, in the role of the "headhunter" I see many examples every day pointing out how crucial (and sometimes damaging) these factors can be to both parties. Therefore I'd like to point out the following:

- Anyone interviewing should always consider and respect the other's point of view and agenda.

- Anyone who has ever been in a position to hire staff knows the choices that are made affect the reputation and creative work of the entire group.

- Anyone looking for work should recognize how important that next job is toward their career development and future employment.

Tables can turn rapidly in business. Everyone should recognize and remember what it means to be in the other's place. Too often we find that our most cooperative applicant becomes the most unnecessarily demanding client or the difficult, inaccessible client turns suddenly into the vulnerable job seeker. Therefore, we should remember what it is to walk in another's shoes, and so:

- Anyone who makes hiring decisions should recognize that the decision-making seat can quickly be turned into the applicant's chair.

Hiring is about choices, priorities, and decisions — and what drives people to make them. It's also about how important these decisions are.

- How the structuring and hiring policies of an office can be the key to its growth.

- How the relationships can be maintained and nurtured for the sharing of success.

- How careers can be nurtured.

- How not to blow an important interview.

- What people in positions of power really want from an employee.

- How reputations can be made or broken.

- How the players commence their dance and, sometimes, why it ends.

The Employer's Viewpoint

Candidates under consideration for a position always ask us what the "feedback" was and often sincerely desire constructive criticism. Most employers do not want to take the time and make the effort to comment constructively. As discussed, if the criticism is negative it's especially distasteful to do so. However, the standard response we receive is: "it's just not right" or perhaps "it's not a fit." Understandably, designers find it hard to face these ambiguous responses. However, the word "fit" does tell a significant story. *Fit means everything.* It relates to everything previously mentioned from "tailoring" a portfolio to meeting client needs and expectations. It also tells more about certain expectations that sometimes are not accurately expressed in job descriptions. The firm is seeking appropriateness.

Let's step back and consider what happens when a company determines they need to hire. The first driving force will be the work load. During the very difficult recession that began in 1989, virtually every company reassessed their employment needs. The majority went through various modes of downsizing, restructuring, or as one corporation put it, re-engineering. The net effect for most corporations is a structure whose work forces are "lean and mean." In many ways it created a healthier work environment with a hallmark of accountability. No company can afford or tolerate individuals who do not have clear responsibility and a rational role. Gone are scores of employees whose roles represented built-in redundancies. The body of the remaining work force is made up of people who are flexible team players, ready to assume a variety of functions. In many cases job descriptions were written to combine jobs or articulate the need for people who were more knowledgeable of the "big picture" and were generally more sophisticated.

The Lean and Mean Workplace

The kind of person who will enter this lean workplace is therefore another key component in the newly augmented hiring criteria. The 1990's has produced a market for the educated talent who is not "just creative." There has been a general acceleration in the past few years for individuals who understand the broader scope of the job, department, or firm. Creative talent must understand the business of the business and recognize that design is only a tool for information in order to communicate a marketing strategy or image.

Who Gets Hired

The question of who gets hired and why is often answered by the ability of creative people to verbally as well as visually articulate these principles. In a very competitive marketplace how and why hiring decisions are made is the critical point of concern. What are employers looking for? What will make them choose one person over another? While we began to explore some of the answers in the preceding paragraph, that is not the whole story. The overriding common thread in job descriptions focuses on personality and the ability to be a team player. Time and again we are requested to find individuals who can not only contribute on the highest level of creativity, but who can contribute to the group as a whole.

It's a constant quest for the "perfect person" who can assume a leadership role (if senior) or have the potential for more responsibility than the position calls for, but can also function as member of the team. Nobody wants high-strung creative egos. I cannot stress how often these same words are repeated by vastly different firms. Strong egos and temperaments are not welcome. No firm wants a disruptive personality within their work group. It is necessary to make clear, however, we are not diminishing the person who has a strong vision or opinions. The key is how opinions are communicated to others.

Work Ethic

Another important criteria is the work ethic. Everyone who is successful (without exception) is highly dedicated to the quality of the product and willing to put in whatever effort is required to make the product as perfect as possible, on time and within budget. This is not an easy objective but a necessary one. In this aspect the fundamental criteria are motivation and quality. The "good" people are manic about quality and are obsessively unrelenting. This all translates into a passion for one's work. While passion can be stimulated by challenge, it cannot be learned and all too few have it. It's a characteristic not readily found but instantly recognized and appreciated. These value-added characteristics and requirements are all in addition to the importance of individual creativity and various technical skills necessary for employment. They are the fundamental deal makers or deal breakers in hiring decisions. These attitudes cannot be communicated through the portfolio. Your portfolio, remember, is just your introduction to a firm. It is the first cut on screening out individuals. It moves you up to the short list. It is during the interview that your attitudes and personality traits must become evident. If the appropriate questions are not being asked, you must aggressively address these issues. You

Summary

must be able to communicate your awareness of business issues, work priorities, and your personal dedication into any conversations about your work or portfolio.

To summarize what employers want, the following is a classical listing of skills and personality requirements made by employers, large and small, when giving my firm a hiring request. It is a time when they can, in candor and off the record, vent their frustrations. I use the word "frustrations," because when looking for work you rarely consider that the employer is often at his or her wit's end trying to find someone with the necessary skills! In any case, the following is a list of characteristic requests made by employers in a majority of current job descriptions for people at different levels of expertise:

- Talent: always first, but never enough by itself.

- Business savvy: innate understanding of the firm's objectives.

- Smart: not just I.Q. but street smarts too.

- Commitment: to quality and the need for perfection.

- Motivation: toward the firm and getting the job done.

- Verbal skills: able to articulate the design process to client and staff alike and participate in client presentations.

- Appearance: looking professional, representing the company. (We have observed many instances in which a candidate got the job because their appearance contributed to the nature of the job and the image of the firm. I need to make the distinction that these are legitimate factors and not those based on sexism.)

- Organizational skills: able to establish priorities, supervise others, control budgets.

- Technology: hands-on or at least an understanding of current computer uses, printing, paper, and production.

- Writing skills: the ability to contribute or originate written proposals.

- Flexibility: no job description can say it all. The ability to roll with the punches, wear whichever hat is necessary, pitch in, do the job, fill the void.

- Attitude: and do it all cheerfully, always working as a team player.

- References: and a general reputation for accountability on the job.

The Candidate's Viewpoint

Impossible requests? Not really. The above list of characteristics defines virtually every successful person I know. While you will not be expected to do it all on your first job, you will at least recognize the road ahead and aspire to those goals. However, you can perhaps understand how difficult it is to find "ideal" employees. As one of my clients stated with a sigh: "Good people are not difficult to find — they're impossible to find!"

Well, what about the other side of this equation? What do designers want when they are looking for work? Why do they want to leave a job? What's going wrong? Why are they frustrated too? The following is a listing of motivating factors I've observed though the years:

- Professional growth: People will either not take a job or will leave if professional growth is blocked by others in the company.

- Quality of clients: Designers recognize that the level or nature of the work will affect their future work. They want to work for an organization that will defend good creative work and fight for the right decisions.

- Need for diversity: Most designers desire a variety in their work experience. Sometimes they may leave a specialized job after a while to find diversity or move toward another goal.

- Recognition: A common frustration is the failure of employers to recognize effort. This recognition may be demonstrated in traditional ways with title and money, but often the lack stems from a very personal need for the "pat on the back."

- Money: What a job is worth is the crux of this issue. The financial realities of the marketplace and questions of employee value are the heart of the problem. Salaries differ substantially due to the size of the firm, the nature of the work, the geographical location and the cost of living. Some firms pay what they think they can get away with, and some what they think they have to. Some corporate salaries are tightly scheduled by restrictive compensation scales often determined and evaluated by outside compensation consultants. These salaries are scheduled within a range allocated to the job description and do not allow for much flexibility or negotiation. Employees sometimes have erroneous ideas of their worth or perhaps no idea at all if they have been working at one place for a long time. However, this is of key importance when accepting a position or leaving one. See Chapter 12: "The Money Question."

- Lifestyle: There seems to be a newer outlook on the meaning and form a quality lifestyle can take in the 1990's. In contrast to the 80's, many individuals are focusing on family and the amount of leisure time available. Therefore the relevant issues of length of commute, amount of overtime, holidays, vacation time, and relocation to other geographical environments arise. The need to put in unusual overtime is often a reason for leaving a job or not taking it.

- Opportunity: The best reason to take a job is opportunity and the best reason to leave a job is lack of opportunity. For the ambitious, nothing replaces the ability to realize one's goals. We have seen many individuals make a lateral move (accepting the same salary) as well as step back (take less) in title and salary because the new job was perceived as an opportunity to move forward.

- Position: Often the way to move up is by moving out. It is very common to leave a job because of a logical need to change responsibilities, title and/or salary The individual can feel blocked in his or her present job because of the structure of the firm (for example, it can be too small or too large to offer the next step up). Or perhaps there is someone in that coveted job who is not going to leave, or the employer does not recognize the need for promotion. The complaint is often "There's just no place to go!"

- Women's Issues: The demographics of design are heavily weighted towards women. For reasons not

The New Feminine Majority

completely clear, Graphic Design is overwhelmingly female for those under 40 years old. Employers will need to accommodate women who want a family and a career. While there is a slow movement toward flexible hours (flex time) and maternity leave (for men too), at the time of this writing it is strictly token (See Benefits, Chapter 9). Talented women will not want to accept positions not offering maternity leave. Several have indicated the desire for four-day work weeks. This picture is a changing one and I feel will play a stronger role in hiring issues as this work force matures.

There are other hiring factors to consider in any discussion of women in graphic design.

(1) Women are not always paid as much as men. Sometimes the cause falls at the feet of women. They simply do not ask for as much money. This may be caused by a lack of security or lack of aggressive negotiation skills. I'm not sure. However, this condition will certainly change, since time is on the side of a maturing and growing female work force. They will be assuming the senior positions of the future.

(2) As the world economy grows, many positions focus on extended travel. This can be difficult for those with young families.

(3) Many employers are in open admiration of and court the woman in the marketplace. If you refer back to our employers' wish list, you'll note the emphasis on flexibility and verbal skills. Women seem to excel in these areas. Perhaps it's because they are raised to assume so many roles and wear all those hats? In any case, savvy employers recognize these important traits.

- Harassment: Simply put, harassment exists and can take many forms. When possible, and when it's recognized, most people will change jobs rather than try to make a change in the workplace. Harassment can be physical (unusual work loads or extra-long hours), sexual, racial or psychological (applying unnecessary pressure, destroying self-confidence). The protagonist is usually playing power politics or is simply a tyrant or bully. Some employers have been classified as "screamers" or "throwers" by people we have interviewed. A warning light would be an unusually high rate of turnover for employees in the firm. When too many employees come and go, some firms get reputations for being "revolving doors," and, while it can be for other reasons, subtle or overt harassment may be one cause.

The Interview It's obvious, when considering the employer's and candidate's priorities as noted above, the interview is a critical session in which a great deal of substantive information needs to be communicated by both parties. Unfortunately, few people have extensive interviewing experience and personnel or human resource professionals can be jaded by doing too much interviewing. Often what a person is saying and what they are thinking can vastly differ. However, the person who recognizes the variety of dynamics in play has an advantage and a better opportunity to get his or her message communicated as accurately as possible. Let's look at some methods to create the best platform of communication.

- Be prepared: Like the Boy Scout motto, always be prepared. Do "due diligence." In business jargon this means make the effort to properly research the project. Research as much as you can about the firm

**Preparation
and Timing**

before your interview. Find out who their clients are. Find out what kind of work they specialize in (if any) and who is responsible for hiring. Find out who you will ultimately report to either before or during the interview. Recognize that the person interviewing you may only be able to make recommendations and not have the authority to hire you.

- Additional portfolio material: Based on your information you may want to bring along additional material pertinent to their needs, perhaps additional sketches. You might also consider bringing personal artwork (illustration, photography, etc.) and ask if the interviewer would like to see it. Be sure to offer this work as an optional consideration. Do not be put off if the interviewer doesn't have time or isn't interested.

- Timing: Be punctual. Allow yourself some extra time if you're not sure how long it will take to get there. Check out your transportation options ahead of time, not at the last minute.

Personal Style

- Attire: Dress in a professional manner. Every company has its own "culture" which dictates what is customary attire. Even if dress is very casual, you won't make a mistake by dressing for the interview and if you have only one interviewing suit, this is the time to wear it. When you are there you'll probably see how others dress and get a better idea of what it would be like for you inside the company. We knew one person who went to the office building a day or two before her interview and watched people leaving for lunch to see how they dressed. Another person we know took the subway on a hot New York day so as

Regional Styles

not to sit down and wrinkle her dress before an interview. She was meeting with a famous designer known for fashion and fragrance and knew her appearance was critical. This behavior is not silly or compulsive. It's smart.

The issue of "style" is the critical point. Style requirements can range from the high fashion image of a New York cosmetic firm to the conservative Midwest corporation who believe a woman should not wear a pantsuit to an interview. It may seen unfair and perhaps sexist, but in today's world it is a fact of life. Style can mean the trendy New York or Los Angeles design studio whose dress code is based on Soho or Melrose Avenue. Style can also mean marketing communications firms and corporations that regard expensive, well-tailored suits with discreet accessories as the norm. Often I feel life is one big costume party and you have to decide which party you wish to attend. However, to deny the impact of these factors would be naive and ultimately close off opportunities. Lastly, the way you dress sends an important message to others in the same way good manners do. It says something about how you feel about your own image, possibly about the future you crave, and how you perceive the needs of your future employer. The bottom line of this subject is that people really do lose jobs and opportunities based on their appearance and personal presentation.

- Beginning: The old adage is that you have 30 seconds to make an impression. The way you say hello and shake hands says a great deal. Look people in the eye. The inability to sustain eye contact reveals personal

**First
Impressions**

insecurities or hidden agendas. I know at least two
people who lost opportunities directly because of this
factor. The employers expressed a feeling of "being
uncomfortable" with someone who didn't offer direct
eye contact. Some people, aware of the need for a
firm, positive handshake as a sign of character, can
nearly break one's hand. I always feel they have read
some self-help book and taken it too much to heart.
On the other hand (no pun intended) it's also surprising how many limp, damp handshakes I get. The
bottom line is: Be yourself, be as relaxed as possible,
and know that nonetheless someone is sizing you up
instantly (and that person may be equally nervous).
As an yoga practitioner, whenever I feel tense, I
always try to breathe deeply, clear my mind of extra-
neous subjects as much as possible, and take heart in
the fact that the person I'm going to meet is just
another human being with many of the same insecurities as anyone. Be pleasant, respectful and polite; ask
where they would like you to sit, if it's not obvious.
Try to think of this person as a *professional friend*.
Think of yourself as being on the same side, as if you
are already a part of their team and share the same
objectives. Do not overstep your bounds.

**Dynamics of
Communication**

- Listening and responding: Let the person interviewing
  you take the lead and direct the conversation, as least
  in the beginning. There are likely to be plenty of
  opportunities for you to ask questions, so *practice the
  art of listening*. The ability to listen to another person
  and concentrate on what he or she is really saying
  (and sometimes what they think they are saying) is a
  very important trait. This is true not only in the

interview, but throughout your business activities. Too often candidates are too intent on what they are going to say to listen to the interviewer. This may be because of nerves. If you listen carefully and address points the other person raises, your communication will be focused to that individual's criteria. You'll be able to direct your answers in a germane manner. It's surprising how few people know how to listen. We even get this quality listed as part of a job description. The request, "I want someone who knows how to listen" is not uncommon. If you're worried about remembering all your questions, bring along a written list. It's perfectly acceptable.

Keeping Momentum

- Breaking appointments: Obviously this is something to avoid as it complicates situations and may send a negative message. In the first place, scheduling interviews can be a difficult task when it involves people with busy schedules who perhaps travel a great deal. Sometimes interviews are with more than one person and those schedules have to be coordinated. Changing appointments is acceptable when there is an understandable and therefore an acceptable reason. The risk is losing the "timing" or momentum of the opportunity. However, if it becomes a pattern, it can mean a loss of interest (perhaps for both parties). If you are not feeling well and not "up" for an interview, the best course is to postpone. Many interviews have been "blown" because the person was not functioning at full speed. If you decide to go to the meeting be sure to tell them why you are not up to par, that you didn't want to cancel and request to come back at another time.

**Expect the
Unexpected
Question**

- Classic Interview Questions: These are some common questions and topics you should be prepared to encounter. Every interviewer, naturally, has his or her own style of conducting an interview. Some are relaxed, some interrogatory. Remember, no matter how relaxed the atmosphere may be, it's a time for testing.

(1) Why are you planning to leave your job and/or why are you interested in this firm? We have discussed many logical and appropriate reasons. Now is the time for you to be prepared to articulate them. Never, however, say anything negative or damaging about you last or current employer.

(2) Future goals: Be prepared for questions about how you perceive your future. This can be a dangerous trap. If you view this job as a temporary stage in your life, do not say so. The employer wants to know that if you are hired you will be there for a considerable and fair period of time. Understand that the first three to six months of your employment is probably going to involve a learning curve. The employer is investing in you and wants a reasonable return. We had one memorable time when a corporation flew a designer from coast to coast after initial interviews in his home city. Early on in the interview at corporate headquarters he was asked the famous and standard "personnel" question, "What is your five-year goal?" His response was to have his own business. He was out the door soon after that answer, and the interviewer immediately picked up the phone to call me.

(3) Personal Traits: Be prepared to answer questions that attempt to identify your personal tastes and

beliefs. Who do you most admire? What has been a motivating force in your life? What books do you read? When was the last time you were in a museum? Where do you like to vacation? Questions that would be considered strictly personal (for example, intimate family details, such as plans to get married or have a baby, or about politics, sex, or age) are illegal. Therefore these questions are designed to learn more about your personality and character. Employers are usually seeking a well-rounded individual with a variety of personal interests.

How to Show Motivation

- Motivation: Your personal motivation toward this position will be a key element in your interview. The entire manner of your participation in the interviewing process points to the level of your motivation, including your promptness, dress, etc. You need to articulate the level of your interest in the firm, job, and career opportunity; as well as the manner in which you are accustomed to working and your energy level. Basically you want to communicate to your future employer that you will welcome the opportunity to participate in the business, giving 110% of your talent, skills, energy, and ability.

- Lunch/Dinner/Drinks: Part of your interviewing process may include some time in a restaurant. There are several objectives to this kind of activity that are very important. They all relate to you as a thinking individual, to your manners and how you conduct yourself publicly.

(1) While it is excellent to give both of you the chance for a less formal, relaxed meeting and to get to know

each other, remember it is still part of the testing process. Knowing this, it is your task to show a relaxed, self-confident manner.

Manners and Mannerism

(2) Being in a restaurant gives your future employer the opportunity to observe you in the surroundings in which business is often conducted. Your deportment, table manners and level of sophistication would all impact on your relationships with your clients. How you make "small talk" and how you move on to the business issues are part of the game. If you happen to be ordering first, try not to order a drink unless your host does. A majority of people today don't drink at lunch. You want to keep your wits about you anyway. Let your host be dominant, calling for the waiter, asking for the check. If you have checked your coats and are not paying for the meal it is proper for you to tip the coat room attendant.

- Questions to ask:

What You Need to Know

(1) Find out what is the organizational structure of the firm.

(2) Find out who you will report to and who will make the hiring decision. It may not be the same person who is conducting the interview.

(3) Ask if other interviews will be necessary and who you will be meeting with. Find out their title so you'll understand their position within the structure of the firm.

(4) Try to find out how long they have been looking for someone. If the job is open too long there may be a problem.

(5) Find out if it's a new position or a replacement. If it's a replacement it's always helpful to know why the person left; however, it may be a difficult question to ask. If it's a new position, carefully check out their expectation level regarding the job description. Often descriptions change on new positions because the employers may not have thought everything out thoroughly. New positions can often mean a better opportunity. It's also easier not to follow in another's footsteps.

(6) Ask when they plan to make a hiring decision and when they need someone to start. It is sometimes possible to find out how many people they are considering (giving you an idea of what the competition is like).

(7) Ask if you can see samples of their work. Remember what they do will go into your portfolio and affect your next position.

Trial Projects

- Freelance and projects: Indicate you're available for freelance if it's possible for you to do so. Sometimes employers like to suggest a trial project as a test. If so, be sure to get as complete a briefing as possible of the nature of the project. You'll often be gaged against currently employed designers who may have the advantage of understanding the clients better. You should always be paid for any work you do. If you do work ask if a purchase order is required so that you don't fall into "accounting limbo" and not get paid. If you do a project, make sure you deliver it on time.

- Salary: Toward the end of the interview your should ask what the firm is planning to pay for the position. However, you will probably be asked first what your

**How to
Express Your
Financial
Needs**

salary expectations are. This may even come as a
response to your question. Remember, salary is only a
base. It must be viewed in the context of a whole
package with benefits. This will be discussed in
greater detail in Chapter 12: The Money Question.
For the purpose of this section, understand that it is an
issue to be dealt with during the interview. This is
always a difficult, sensitive moment if you don't have
any prior information. Several options include:

(1) Telling your current salary and indicating you
expect more (factors may include that you haven't
been given an expected raise, the firm is having financial problems, you are up for a raise but your want to
leave anyway for stated reasons).

(2) That money is not your reason for wanting this
position and you'd feel better knowing how they
evaluate your worth within their company.

(3) Indicating a range that you feel comfortable with,
without using specific numbers, such as high $20's,
low to mid $30's, etc.

(4) That this will be your first job and the opportunity
is your foremost consideration (however, you still
need to make a living.) With regard to first jobs, please
remember it's going to cost your employer to train
you. You should always think of your first couple of
positions as continuing education. Salaries are far less
negotiable with corporations. You probably would be
in discussion with a member of the Human Resources
Department who would be working with clear-cut
schedules or guidelines.

- Concluding the interview: Make sure you understand the next phase of the interviewing process. Are you to get back in touch or will they contact you? Do they want any other materials from you? Do not fall into the trap of calling them too often. The ball will be in their court and you have to take their lead. Sometimes firms are too polite, don't know how to say no, and may lead a person on unnecessarily. When you leave, say "Thank you." Get the person's business card if possible and send a thank you note if you're not coming back soon. Get the title and spelling correct on the note. If this is a position you are anxious to have, express that motivation in a note or letter. Tell the person responsible for hiring how much you want the job, why you believe you have much to offer and how you would devote all your energies to the company. Strong motivation is a major factor in hiring decisions and you have nothing to lose by assuming an aggressive stance.

Maintaining Continuity

Confidentiality and Non-Compete Agreements

You may be asked to sign a letter or contract relating to the proprietary business of the firm. It could also involve non-compete agreements should you leave the firm. Just understand that this is common practice among many design firms and the number of firms attempting to restrict departing employees is on the rise. Since the structure of these contracts can greatly vary and they could hamper your future ability to be employed, it is absolutely necessary not to sign anything without first showing it to an attorney.

Psychological Testing

There are many types of tests to qualify different kinds of information. A small percentage of corporations use these devices. Your decision to accept taking the test is strictly voluntary, but may be a condition attached to getting the job.

Medical Examinations

Passing a medical exam is a reasonably common practice among corporations but not consultant firms. It may also be necessary if there is an insurance policy attached to the benefits package. The last few years have seen a rise in drug and HIV testing as well. It is possible you maybe asked for a blood or urine sample. Several Wall Street firms we know will "spring" a urine test on an applicant during one of the interviewing appointments without forewarning. These tests can pick up traces of marijuana or a poppyseed bagel digested three days before the test. Needless to say you won't be penalized for eating bagels.

References

You should always be ready to offer references, if requested. If you have letters of reference, bring them to the interview. You can ask the interviewer if he or she would like to have a copy, but it may or may not be necessary. References are generally requested in the last stage of candidate selection just before an offer is extended. At that time it is common practice to present three references. Usually, if you are still employed, it is not possible to get a reference from your current employer. In that case seek references from a confidant in your office or someone you reported to at another office. Other likely references would be people who you supervised, those who you dealt with as vendors (photographers, illustrators, suppliers) and anyone else who could speak about your ability to follow instructions, supervise others, meet deadlines, hold to budgets, and the like. References should be as recent as possible and no more than three to four years past. When your future employer is calling your references personally, be sure to allow time for you to alert them to expect the call (and therefore double-check that are available).

Accepting or Rejecting an Offer

Accepting an offer is a fairly uncomplicated affair. If you are not presently working, you need only find out when the firm wishes you to start. Perhaps first you'll need to fulfill a freelance obligation. Remember though, if you have any work obligations, finishing them is professionally correct no matter how much pressure is placed on you by your new employer. Never walk away from a promise. Your future employer wouldn't want you to do it to him or her either, and perhaps she or he may need that as a reminder. For some reason, once employers have made up their minds to hire they often want the instant gratification of having the employee on premises immediately. If you have to leave a position, you'll have to do so in the same professional manner in which you conduct all your business dealings. We'll cover that subject in some detail in Chapter 13, "Moving On — How To Leave A Job."

Rejecting an offer is a matter of diplomacy. Your reasons for rejecting a position can be many and show an exercise in sound judgement. However, it's important to remember that an employer faces your rejection with about the same distaste as you would feel being rejected by a firm you wanted to join. As always, it's important to consider how it is for the other person. The employer has made a decision based on the whole hiring procedure. Perhaps it was very time-consuming. He or she now has to start all over again. Significantly, you may want to "leave the door open" for future opportunities with that firm, or simply understand that as individuals who move about in an industry, you may meet again. The effect is the same. You need to reject the offer with grace and professionalism. Thank them for the opportunity the offer represents and give a reasonably clear understanding of why you are not accepting. Do not in any way insult them or their firm with your rejection. If you don't like their work, find

A Matter of Diplomacy

another reason. Only raise the issue of insufficient salary if you would accept the job for more money, for they may come up with a better offer. Tell them the truth if you have another offer you feel is superior. The reason (such as working conditions, growth opportunity, benefit package) may be constructive. Just keep in mind that you may meet again.

Summary

In summary, let's consider the whole picture of the hiring process. Your portfolio is the access to the firm, the foot in the door to determine whether your creative point of view and talent are appropriate to the firm's business core. The next stage in this process centers around you as a person. All the criteria listed really focus on what you are about. Your personality, attitude, upbringing, and goals come into play as critical components. The last phase relates to whether you determine this position is the right direction for the long term. If the firm is of like mind, it will make an offer. I've referred to the synergistic relationship between employee and employer as a dance for two. It is a partnership of the first order of importance. Every combination of personalities is unique in every sense of the word. Situations never quite duplicate. (That is what makes my work so fascinating.) I always advise, when the decision to accept or reject is most difficult, to listen to that small internal voice within you. Sometimes it's just a "feeling" in the pit of your stomach. Contemplate, listen, but don't fear risk. Nothing is achieved without it.

The Money Question

12 alary requirements are probably the most difficult matter for the average person to negotiate. Compounding the issue is the perception that salary negotiations are essentially an extremely distasteful process to be avoided if at all possible. And because it's so subjective, most designers practice avoidance, diminishing their earning capability. The negotiating process with its resulting salary package is, of course, the essential ingredient of any employment contract. Negotiation is an art form not taught as part of any design curriculum. In addition we are again confronted with the issue of choice. How can you negotiate if you don't know what the possibilities and choices are?

Salary Variables: What Are You Worth?

You are in an interview, you really want the position and you are asked what your salary requirements are. How do you respond? It is always easier to be passive and respond to a number offered, but the blatant act of firmly stating a number you want is often very difficult. Perhaps it's the whole issue of assigning a number as an indication of one's worth. It's putting a price on your head. Are you secure and forthright or do you hedge knowing that you'll take any reasonable offer?

How do you establish your worth as a creative person? How do you price creativity? The aspect of general financial ignorance plays an important role in this process because many designers simply don't know what they are worth in the marketplace or what the market will bear. This information is hard to come by. The only gauges are occasional salary surveys like the ones published by the AIGA (American Institute of Graphic Arts). To inquire about the most recent survey contact AIGA, 1059 Third Avenue, New York, NY 10022.

Surveys

"Street-Wise" Information

Newspaper ads are also a market-wise indication of current salary offerings; however, many ads use the ambiguous phrase "salary is competitive" or "commensurate with experience." It certainly leaves the person applying for that job at a disadvantage. Some salary information is hearsay or of the classic "grapevine" variety. Within a few companies there is often a "feeling" or underground knowledge by the staff of how much various employees earn. But more often, especially in a larger firm, individuals are operating in the dark with little knowledge of what their colleagues or counterparts earn. Friends are little help for few want to confide how much they earn.

Employers usually assume one of two opposing positions regarding releasing income information. One is to create parity between employees (probably recognizing as well that eventually there are few secrets in firms), the other is that all financially related information is proprietary and strictly confidential.

Counter Offers

Employees sometimes embark on job searches just to learn what they can earn by making a move, and use that information to negotiate an increase with their employer. I have always felt that is a form of blackmail and I wouldn't be happy staying with a firm who would only acknowledge my real worth at the equivalent of gunpoint. It's my opinion that the employee is never perceived the same way again, by the employer or by his or her colleagues in the workplace who usually end up knowing the whole story. Counter offers are reasonably common, however, and some feel it's a better course of action than making a move to another firm and therefore into the unknown. It becomes a matter of personal business philosophy and must be dealt with on a case by case basis. Also, there are many firms that will, on principle, never make a counter offer.

**Establishing
a Realistic
Picture**

What is the best way to overcome this lack of information and find a reasonable path toward salary equity? Once again the responsibility for the research effort falls on the designer's shoulders. If you want a realistic picture, it is necessary to utilize the above-mentioned sources and try to make a personal survey. Professional recruiters, like those at my firm, are probably one of these best sources for this confidential information. In fact, our firm is such an excellent barometer of the marketplace and of salaries around the country that we are often asked to advise our clients on what they need to pay. In some instances we work as consultants to design firms and corporations who need our expertise on comparative and equitable compensation scales. In addition we have developed a survey which we distribute at various speaking engagements. You will find that survey at the end of this chapter. Some contributing factors in gauging salaries are:

**Contributing
Factors**

- Regional: Questions of location are very important. The cost of living and cost of overhead will influence pay scales. There are distinct differences in salary levels in New York, Los Angeles, Atlanta, or Seattle.

- Economic: Salaries can reflect a buyer's or seller's market. Wages will be affected by recessions or what firms will be willing to pay for premium talent. Then there are regional factors. The boom and then dry periods Texas has experienced through the 1980's and 1990's would be an excellent example.

- Size: Small firms generally have smaller budgets if smaller companies comprise their client base. Size of the firm is only meaningful when considered in relation to their client base. There are many small firms (under 20 people) who have high-profile clients and therefore command parity in fees with large firms.

Company Variables

- The Type of Firm: Studios and marketing communications firms may not have the same budgets as large corporations. But it is difficult to generalize because there are exceptions for every rule. One must consider that the major differences between corporate versus non-corporate positions are in the areas of benefits and freedom to negotiate. Corporate benefits are usually far more expansive (see benefits) than a private firm can offer. Corporate salaries are another matter. They are usually formulated on a sliding scale set to gauge levels of experience and the quality of responsibility defined in the job description. Corporate salaries will thus be graded and pegged to titles with a high and low range. Corporations like to hire at the low to medium range, leaving room for salary increases through the years of employment. Should the individual reach the top of the range, their only recourse to future salary growth would be a change in job description and title. With such firm guidelines it is easy to understand that negotiating a salary with a corporation is far more restrictive than a group based on an entrepreneurial business mode.

- Specialization: Different areas of business command higher fees. Two extreme examples would be feature films and book design. The entertainment field offers much higher compensation than book publishing. Since creative people are often driven by what they enjoy doing in contrast to where the most money can be earned, this information will be more important to some that others. However, it is at least important to understand what the possibilities can be when making life choices. The Salary Survey at the end of this chapter points out some of the differentials.

What's Your Job Worth?

A controlling element in setting salaries is the amount of business particular design projects can generate. The greater the financial impact of the product and its ability to persuade sales the greater the financial rewards. With that principle clarified it's easy to understand why an advertising creative director can realize a salary of perhaps a quarter to half million dollars, which is far more that any designer would hope for. Consider the amount of money at stake in the placement of a television commercial scheduled to air during a Super Bowl broadcast. Consider the cost of airing the commercial ($850,000 for 30 seconds in 1992), the cost of production in making it and the financial and image risk to the corporate sponsor. With all that at stake, is any one going to quibble about how much it will cost to hire the best talent?

The higher the stakes for image and sales, the larger the compensation for doing the job right. It's easy to understand. As we have discussed, within the design field we have companies which have various specialities. The associated expertise contributes to set the value of their services. They are experts who will be compensated more than generalists. A comparison to health care is not unfounded. A general practitioner will usually charge less for an office visit than a specialist. Design firms or agencies creating movie advertising, title treatments, and trailers find themselves in a particularly richly compensated, if volatile, area. Firms specializing in identity, whether corporate, branding, or retail, are at the higher end of the compensation scale. After all, how often is a corporation going to change its identity? Think of the impact of that new system. Packaging design can also hold great importance as it directly contributes to sales at the point of sale. Book design, while hardly insignificant, has the least effect as most people will buy a book for other reasons than its appearance (thus, they don't judge a book by its cover.) Editorial designers have direct impact on a magazines' image and sales. One look at a newsstand, with all those covers screaming for your attention, will confirm that the magazines' appearance contributes to the message "buy me!" The interior spreads continue to reinforce the magazines' content, message, and legibility.

Benefit Packages

Many benefits and perks are available, and can drastically change from one firm to another. The best option is to know what could possibly be available versus what the standard package is for a company. Then see if there is any room to negotiate. A large corporation with a rather complete package may indeed offer most items while small design firm may offer just a few. The following is not a complete listing, but will give you an idea of some of the potential opportunities to add to compensation.

- Health Insurance: This has become the most costly area for employers. The explosion in health insurance costs over the past few years has, in many cases, required employers to seek other methods of coverage. HMO's or organized health plans offering a selected group of physicians are gaining in popularity. Many firms have raised the deductible base and/or have made their plans contributory. This means that the employee must assume some of the costs. The percentages vary from firm to firm. While some form of medical insurance is standard practice for most offices, dental insurance is not as commonly available. Most medical plans cover psychiatric care in a modest way but do not give it the same benefit scale as other physicians. However, one of this country's top corporations operates a sanitarium exclusively for its employees. (Perhaps this is an interesting message about the cost of "making it" in America.)

- Health Clubs: In recognition of the long-term benefits of a healthy employee, many large corporations will have on-site health clubs or gyms. Some firms will offer memberships in commercial health club facilities. For some senior individuals a country club membership is a negotiable point.

- Vacations, Holidays, Personal, and Sick Days: This category is self-explanatory and can vary from one firm to another to a great extent. The ability to "buy" an additional week of vacation is a newer option offered by some firms. "Buying" can mean approved leave without pay or earning "time credits" with unused sick day allowances.

- Leave of Absence: This can be negotiated on a case by case basis. Most firms do not have specific policies in place.

- Life and Disability Insurance: Most major medical policies include a life insurance plan equal to one year's income. Senior level personnel can often negotiate an increased life insurance benefit as well as disability insurance.

- Expense Accounts: Travel and entertainment expenses that are directly related to the firm's business are paid directly or reimbursed by the company. It is possible to be given a guaranteed annual amount as a perk. However, all such expenditures have to be documented with receipts.

- Company Transportation: Many firms will offer a company car to senior level employees. Often it is a negotiable item and the make of the car becomes a status symbol recognizing the seniority of the employee. Sometimes the negotiation surrounding the make of car can be tense, for the significance lies in the message sent to the rest of the firm regarding the person's status. Monthly auto rentals can also be part of the package when a firm needs an employee to travel as part of the job. It can also be a factor if the firm is in a fairly inaccessible location for the employee they wish to hire. Company vans, buses, and airplanes are occasionally available as necessary.

- Commutation: If the office location is considered a lengthy distance to commute, the firm may offer to pay these expenses.

- Pension plans: There are several plans available, all of which operate on the same principle of placing money into holding accounts for retirement before paying taxes on those funds. Common plans are the 401K and SEP-IRA. These plans can be payroll deductions, employer's contributions or a combination of contributions by the employees and employers. Some plans stipulate a period of time to become vested. This means you cannot be eligible to receive the funds unless you stay with the firm for a specific number of years. There maybe a sliding scale of eligibility. For example, after 5 years of employment a 50% vestment; after 6 years 60%, etc. The advantage of all these plans, regardless of your age, is that they become a form of forced savings and/or additional monies to your base salary that are not taxable. They work as the common IRA. The money accrued in the plan is not taxable until you receive it.

- Education: Some firms offer continuing education benefits, reimbursing you for all or part of your expenses. Most plans will only cover educational programs germane to your profession. Some plans will have coverage for family members.

- Seminars and Conferences: Since these are also considered to be educational, many firms, on request, will pay these expenses. They have added-value as vehicles for making new contacts for the firm and as a general internal public relations effort.

- Company Stock: Stock or stock options are available on a case by case basis. Keep in mind there are many ways of offering stock and many grades of stock. Stock as well as profit sharing is used as a form of equity in the firm.

- Profit Sharing: Some firms distribute a percentage of their profits to employees as an incentive. The incentive is to have a vested interest in the general welfare of the company and contribute to its profitability. Obviously the numbers will change from year to year but the system is an excellent method of insuring the employee's role within the company.

- Bonuses: The bonus is totally optional. It can be a year-end or semiannual disbursement based on performance and profitability. Remember, since it is a cash award, the money is completely taxable. In addition to the "reward" system bonus, some firms can offer a sign-on bonus as an incentive to attract an individual. For the firm it means a one-time additional charge without changing the salary base.

- Relocation: Most corporations will include a relocation package for individuals who will move to the site of the company. This is most prevalent with companies which are located in cities where there is an insufficient talent pool. However, that does not mean a company will not pay relocation expenses from one major city to another. The obvious fact is no company wants to incur extra expenses, but if the individual has the unique requirements needed, the money will be there. For smaller firms, paying the price of a move is often out of the question. It should be clear that a smaller company will only pay these costs for experienced personnel. Corporations will relocate a junior-level designer when they recruit from art schools. If a person of only a few years' experience wishes to be in a certain geographical region, the best strategy would be to research the firms in the area, perhaps by calling the local chapter of the AIGA (The American Institute of Graphic Arts) or Art Directors Club. Get listings of member firms, contact them directly and ultimately travel to seek the position and be prepared to move yourself. When visiting a new city give yourself enough time, perhaps even allowing time to freelance. It is always frustrating for me to see designers come to New York for 10 days or two weeks and expect to return home with a job offer.

Relocation costs most often include air fare (with perhaps a couple of visits to find a home) the cost of bringing a spouse to see the new city, and actual moving expenses for belongings. It can also include (but not always) temporary residence expenses, furniture storage costs, help finding schools, day care, even a job for the spouse; help with mortgage points, and sometimes assuming the mortgage and sale of the previous home. Sometimes a flat package is offered to cover these costs and sometimes a smaller firm can offer to pay part of the expenses. Remember, in these cases, you must always be able to document your expenses with receipts.

- Child Care: Unfortunately very few firms offer on-site child care or any allowance to pay for outside facilities. The only firms that have moved in this direction are large corporations.

- Flex Time/Job Sharing: While very few firms are actively involved in flex time or job sharing, the concept to accommodate working parents is gaining momentum. Flex time is defined as the right not to work the standard nine to five and to establish hours that are responsive to the needs of working parents. Perhaps there is a need to work a shorter day but to be able to do some work at home. Several firms in New York have given young mothers a computer and modem to work at home and communicate with the studio electronically. This networking capability is adding a new dimension to defining the workplace. Job sharing is another option. Two people share one job, usually overlapping one day to insure a communications flow. Since graphic design is comprised of a vast female majority (and the numbers are growing every year), the ability to control work time individually will without doubt grow in response to the need.

- Employee Handbooks: Most large companies and many small ones have their benefits and policies spelled out in some form of printed material. You should always ask for it. It is a clear indication of what you can expect as the basis of the firm's offerings. However, many of the items listed above can become negotiable points in the hiring procedure. I have indicated the most common areas. It's always helpful to know what's possible. Keep in mind, however, that many perks are not available to junior employees. There is a clear correlation between the perception of value associated with the employee and the amount of rewards a company will offer.

Negotiating a Salary

Again the advantage is with the person who can view the process in a holistic way, understanding the various economic forces at work. Taking a job and negotiating a salary is a complex endeavor and many facets of the opportunity must be weighed against the other. These considerations should include:

- The nature of the position

- The long or short-term goals of the designer

- The quality of the firm and its business agenda

- The areas of specialization (if any)

- Market factors

- Location

- Benefits

Benefit packages, as described above, are extremely important because they represent non-cash or cash-deferred additions to your salary that have the equivalent of cash value based on *after-tax dollars*. This means that the cash value is more that its face value because it is non-taxable income.

The actual negotiation can be informal, friendly, and brief. A scenario can be a casual, "This is what we feel we can offer you," and since the amount is not a surprise and is agreeable, you accept. Other offers can be far more formal and in a "testing" mode. The quality of the negotiation can establish the power relationships that will continue on the job. This is a time in which you want to be sure to conduct yourself in a cautious and professional manner. Be respectful and courteous, no matter what you may think. It is a general rule of thumb to ask for a little more than you expect to get. If you feel there is room to negotiate, on principal, don't accept a first offer.

Formal and Informal Scenarios

A far more common scenario to the one above would be not respond immediately after you receive a offer, but to defer your response a few days. Give yourself time to "sleep on it." This will give you the opportunity to ponder and gain some clarity. Make sure you know all the other factors in addition to base salary when you get the offer. If there is some part of the offer that is not satisfactory, bring it up.

The timing of salary reviews can become an important issue in discussions of this nature. The first stage is to have the firm specify their review policy and its definition. A review usually means an evaluation of work performance and a possible change in compensation based on the review. It can take place at year end or at the anniversary of the employee joining the firm. Sometimes it can take place much earlier. If the amount offered is deemed insufficient you may ask for an earlier review, perhaps within three or six months. We have found this a generally excellent method to negotiate a higher salary with a time limit for the lower salary. The amount of the future increase is usually not determined at the time of hiring, but the review agreement represents an understanding that an increase is possible at a specific time if performance matches expectation. It also affords the employer less risk if the quality of the employee's work and experience is in question.

Everything is Negotiable

The number of items to be negotiated can sometimes be a surprise. The old adage "everything in life is negotiable" may not be completely true, but is a helpful motto. As long as you do not have an arrogant attitude, your loss exposure in trying to change terms is negligible and you have everything to gain. However, I would caution you that in any negotiation, you must concentrate on realistic priorities. For example it would be futile for a designer with two years experience to negotiate a four-week vacation when the standard is two weeks.

Corporations and many firms may confirm the agreement with a written offer stating the terms. Smaller firms may consider a handshake sufficient. Nonetheless, make sure your offer is real and confirmed and not in an exploratory phase. Every now and then we find a designer who believes he or she has a job offer when the employer is really trying to determine if he or she is available at a certain salary. The confusion is easily understandable, but you would not want to quit a job based on an incomplete offer.

Summary

To sum it up, salary packages are always flexible, an ever-shifting set of priorities and goals. The possible combinations of all these components make for a tremendous variety of possibilities. The components of establishing a package that's fair and equitable to both parties rely heavily on what both perceive as fair. Designers are unique in that accepting positions often has little to do with the salary and a great deal to do with the quality of work, the quality of opportunity, and general lifestyle it offers. Perhaps the best advice is to always go with your basic instinct of what is comfortable for you. The bottom line is always an extremely subjective one.

1992 Salary Survey

(for annual starting salaries shown in thousands)

Field	Entry Level Junior	5–8 Years Experience Intermediate	10+Years Experience Senior
Design Firms			
Packaging Design	$23-25	$30-50	(The salary figures for the senior positions listed below apply to each of the Specialties shown on the left.)
Brand & Corporate Design	"	"	
Identity Design	"	"	project directors: $50-65
Environmental Designers	"	"	design directors: $65-80
Product Designers	"	"	creative directors: $75-175+
Annual Report Designer	$23-28	$35-50	
Corporate Literature Design	"	"	
Account Management (Design Firms)			
Marketing/Sales	$25-30	$40-70	$75-175+
Corporations			
Asst. Art Director/Designer	$25-30	$32-50	
Art Directors			$55-80
Creative Director			$75-100
V.P. Creative Director			$85-175+
Editorial			
Asst. Art Director/Designer	$20-30		
Associate Art Directors		$30-45	
Art Directors		$40-55	$50-85
Creative Directors			$75-125 +
Advertising Agency			
Asst. Art Director/Designer	$20+	$35 (no TV)	
Art Directors		$55 (TV)	
TV Stars (Art Directors with major commercial credits)			$200 +
Sales Promotion			
Art Director/Designer	$25-30	$35-50	$50-75
Creative Directors			$85-175 +

Regional Factors: Los Angeles/San Francisco: 10% less

Midwest/South/Northwest: at least 15% less

Note: + means package of perks that significantly changes compensation

Moving On: When and How to Leave a Job

13

No Place to Go Means No Place to Grow

"I t's time." That is the most common response I get when I ask an applicant why they want to look for another job. What does this internal clock signal? What are the signs that mark the moment to embark on such a career-altering process? Most often it means there is "no place to go." The definition of this often-used phrase means the path forward and upward is blocked. It may be blocked by another person who occupies the position you want and that person shows no indication of leaving or being promoted. It may mean the size of the firm and its structure will not allow for a logical progression. It may mean that if you stay in the safety of your present position without being promoted you will stop growing professionally. "No place to go" often means "no place to grow." It's a feeling of reaching a plateau and not being willing to stay there. Now not everyone wants to constantly move up and that's fine. Many reach a position of contentment and comfort and stay in that place for many years. But for the younger person still carving out a future from a collection of experiences or for the person whose ambition is frustrated, "it's time" has a powerful ring. Nonetheless, other reasons exist for making a move. Money can often be a very compelling cause. Supporting a family, buying a home and other personal motivations may cause dissatisfaction with the present work condition. Professional growth being thwarted or not rewarded inspires the need to change. A glance at the "frustrations" list in Chapter 11, The Candidate's Viewpoint, will identify and confirm the many root causes launching the decision to move on. Work environment, lack of recognition, and the desire to move to another city, can all be factors.

How to Quit

For some reason we are often told how to educate ourselves, how to get a job, how to work, how to design, but little is ever said about how to quit. Acting in a responsible and professional manner once you have decided to leave is just as important as your demeanor when entering a new office. How you leave and the impression you make will affect your relationships with the people involved for the rest of your life. And don't think that once you have left a place you have closed that chapter of your life and it's finished. We have discussed how "round" the world is and how closely people keep interacting with each other through the years. There are constant reminders in everyday conversations of how people seem always amazed to meet up with the past. The key factor is never never "burn bridges." It doesn't matter whether you are motivated by a desire to be considered a pleasant and likeable person or because you have the aspiration to maintain your people network. You should never block your access to anyone you might want to see again or have to be with again.

Maintaining Relationships

Maintaining your credibility and your professional relationships will strongly affect your performance in the workplace and your ability for future networking. There is nothing less productive than to leave a bad impression, or leave a place without grace and then find the same individuals working in the same firm with you years later. It happens! It happens with such frequency it pushes the point of plausibility.

You never know when you will need a recommendation, help of any sort, or perhaps even a job from individuals known through previous employment. The bottom line is the fact that paths keep crossing and we have witnessed these scenarios often in this game of professional musical chairs.

Let's consider a few amusing and sometimes not amusing examples. There was the young designer who left a firm with great hostility and anger. She left in a huff, telling her supervisor exactly what she thought of him! (How many times did you only wish for such an opportunity?) You probably can guess the rest of the story. Two jobs later that same supervisor was hired as a creative director in her firm. It was a very uncomfortable situation, saved only by his understanding that people can make mistakes. One person was hired for a three-month temporary position. The employer went out of his way to make an easy transition after the three months by having the person work part-time while looking for another position. As it was also over the Christmas holidays, the employee was still given presents and a small bonus. When the person left she informed the office manager of her last day, but never said one word to the employer, let alone a good-bye. How could she expect a good reference?

How to Say Good-Bye

Knowing how to say good-bye is as important as saying hello. It is critical to say "thank you." You should say thank you for having the opportunity to work and grow, to learn, to partake of whatever the success of the firm represented, to have accepted any gratuities that were given to you, any time that was spent on your behalf and any effort the firm made to train you and allow you to reach the point that you could leave. Firms often recognize when "it's time" as well as you do and do not experience any animosity at your departure. Many times individuals are anxious and perhaps frightened over the imagined confrontation in the act of resigning. The result can be a relief or letdown, and even a humbling experience, to learn that it may not be a big deal. Experienced and seasoned employers acknowledge the natural process of moving on. Your resignation may cause them some disappointment but without question they will find a method of replacing you. Leaving a job is another time when you must exhibit your sophistication with the process and show professional manners and polish. Remember, whatever you may really be thinking is not the issue.

This is also a point of time to understand you may have an employer who truly does not want you to leave and may make a counter offer. It is a time to keep clear focus on your reasons for leaving. If they are purely monetary, the counter offer may have a significance to you. However, remember that few people leave a firm only for reasons of money. Nothing else is really going to change, so beware of promises that cannot be kept. I do not find counter offers flattering or wise in the vast majority of instances. Consider, if your value to the firm is that much greater, why did it take this action for you to get an increase?

And If You're Fired?

Let's face it —it can happen. The recent recession afforded too many people just that unpleasant experience. There are many euphemisms that people use to try to alleviate the negative emotions attached to the words "fired." Some are kind, others represent corporate-speak that can be dehumanizing. So we experience a broad range of explanations of this action. Almost no one ever says "you're fired!" However, whether you have been let go, cut back, re-structured, excessed or re-engineered, the effect is exactly the same.

Unless you were let go for a reason there is little stigma attached to being fired. The process of firms paring down is all too common and acceptable. Many design firms float on insufficient capitalization, so if a client is lost, cash flow is immediately threatened. Agencies can have "Black Fridays" when a major account leaves, forcing them to immediately fire large numbers of people. Corporations are the slowest to react to a slowdown in revenues and will usually first seek to cut staff by attrition. When they restructure it is usually at the middle management level. When interviewing, simply tell the truth.

Defining the Reason

If you were let go for a reason you have a significantly different problem. Initially you will have to present a logical reason. Most often we are confronted with explanations referring to a "difference of opinion" or "creative conflict" or simply company politics. Whenever you are faced with a problem of describing internal company conflicts be very general and beware of offering any libelous information. It could reflect badly on your diplomatic skills. In addition, your remarks could come back to haunt you in the form of a legal action. If you feel you were wrongfully fired and you wish to protest in some manner, do not sign anything during your exit interview. If you are presented with any documents, show it to an attorney first. Your attorney may also advise you not to accept any severance pay.

Severance

Severance pay is often a way of compensating an individual who has been let go. Severance is not mandatory and the amount varies greatly from firm to firm. Most of the time it is based on the number of years you have been a member of the firm and many firms indicate the rules of severance pay in employee handbooks. Nonetheless, if you are not sure, always ask if you are entitled to severance pay or whether the firm would like to consider giving it to you. Often this can be a negotiable item.

Finishing Work in Progress

Leaving also means not leaving unfinished work or leaving the firm with a problem on their hands. You must be conscientious and professional about your assignments and responsibilities. Sometimes you may be pressured by the firm you are joining to come on board as quickly as possible. You may be the end product of a long search and you represent needed relief in their workplace. Their deadlines are their main priority. The proper notice of leaving is at least two weeks. The amount of notice you give your employer can be more or less dependent on work loads and the length of time you have been with the firm. If you have been there less than a year, one week is acceptable. Do not allow pressure to prevent you from finishing your work and/or handing it over to a co-worker. Your new employer wouldn't want you to leave him or her in a lurch either. Nonetheless know that at some point it is important not to drag out the process. We had one unusual example when an employer insisted the individual report immediately to work or lose the job offer. He needed her to join immediately a team on a business trip to Japan. He recognized that if she was not part of the original team, the Japanese would never fully accept her. She was, however, in the middle of a project that she did not feel should be left suddenly. The job offer was about to be rescinded when we were finally able to negotiate a compromise. She went to Japan for two weeks and upon her return finished the other project while working for her new employer part-time.

Obtaining Portfolio Samples

Industry practice dictates you should have accessibility to samples of all your work including projects of which you have participated. It is your responsibility to present your work accurately, indicating the level of your responsibility, especially should the project be a shared one. Before and when you leave a firm you are entitled to be given samples of your work for your portfolio, barring confidentiality restrictions if products have not yet been released to the public. Some employers can make it difficult, and while there are no legal regulations per se (with the exception of proprietary or confidential projects), common past business practice indicates your entitlement to examples of your past experiences.

Upon exiting a firm, therefore, there may be recent samples you should be sure to request. You probably had updated your portfolio in order to seek employment, but don't forget to collect your most current samples. Perhaps it's new work that's at the printer and you will have to return in order to get them. You may have been working on sensitive projects that cannot be released until they are marketed. Make sure you get them later. These details are easily forgotten in the excitement of change and often are only remembered when you next seek a job and realize you require them for your book. By then it's probably too late. Always protect yourself by keeping an archive of your work history (with duplicates) up to date.

Exit Interviews

A segment of the departing process may be an "exit interview." It may be with a human resource person or with your boss. It should be a time of reflection and constructive evaluation. It may include a written questionnaire. The purpose is two-fold. First, it will give you tools in your search for a new job (if you are being let go) and second, it will allow you to evaluate the company from your point of view. If handled properly, it should give the firm an insight into their dealings with employees.

References

It is a very good idea to ask for a letter of reference upon departure. If you are leaving for another position, you may feel it's a moot point. It's a legitimate request in any case and may turn out to be handy for the future.

Vacations

The luxury of a vacation, be it short or long, between jobs is a terrific advantage. The physical and psychological breather refreshes your outlook and revitalizes your energy level. Of course not everybody can take advantage of this possibility, but consider it an option. Every vacation day you can squeeze into your demanding schedule is a boon. Some individuals prefer to quit after a vacation period or after a bonus period.

This is manipulative but not surprising behavior. It is always questionable to me. If you want to factor in these often deserved and earned benefits then do so, but don't quit immediately, at least for appearance's sake.

Giving Notice

While you may want to give the customary two weeks, notice, in some cases quitting may mean you'll leave before the day is out. In some specialized areas, especially packaging design, the proprietary nature of the work takes precedence over time considerations. Once you have made your intentions to leave known don't be surprised if you find yourself out the door as fast as possible. The sensitivity of the projects have to be protected immediately, especially if the designer is moving to another competitor. In that case the two weeks' notice is forgotten and you will be wished good luck and told to pack up and leave. For the uninitiated it can be a rude shock. It can offer you a forced vacation or you may find yourself starting your new position sooner than expected.

Confidentiality Agreements

After you have left be careful not to talk about your former employer in a negative manner or discuss the confidential qualities of their work. If you had signed a confidentiality agreement, read it again carefully. Make sure you adhere to its restrictions. Whether you signed an agreement or not, the work you did at your former work premises is considered confidential as are the work procedures. Keep in mind that certain knowledge is proprietary and you must not abuse that responsibility. If you do so, in some extreme cases, you might be liable for a lawsuit under clauses relating to "trade secrets."

So you have remembered your professional and personal manners and you are leaving with your reputation intact along with your employer's good wishes for your future. It's a wonderful, exciting time. There is an element of risk as you assume new responsibilities and have to learn to work with a different set of personalities within a different company culture. But life is moving on — *and so are you!*

What Kind of Training Is Needed?

14

One of the first questions we ask when a young designer calls our office looking for a job, is what school he or she attended. It's not a question of whether the designer has a degree but a question of where that degree was obtained, because the content and quality of design education is significantly different from one institution to another. For us it may mean the difference between scheduling an immediate interview or asking the designer to drop off his or her portfolio. This is a clear indication of how significant the quality of education is for the designer in the job market.

General Characteristics of Design Education

Simply put, a common syllabus for graphic design education does not exist in the colleges of United States. Design is a creative process, and therefore, completely subjective. Design education is dependent, upon the vision and insights of those who are responsible for hiring faculty and structuring curriculum and its content. Each institution teaches design from a somewhat different point of view. To confirm this, one only has to examine the portfolios of graduating students. The educational focus and graphic style of these portfolios are, in most instances, so distinctive, it is possible to identify the graduate's college just by looking at them. It is easy to understand how selecting a college could very well enhance or limit future career choices.

Since design programs are different, let us look at some of the primary paths and choices. Initially we need to acknowledge that almost every university has an art department; however, those departments' curricula focus on the traditional of fine arts, such as, drawing, painting, print making, and sculpture. Our analysis here is limited to "professional" programs — the education required to enter the graphic design field. Since the field is so competitive, it is necessary to value and evaluate the pressure put on graduates seeking their first job. We have acknowledged in previous chapters the importance of those first career steps, and how every advantage can help. The educational process is, naturally, the fundamental preparation for those first steps.

An Idiosyncratic Curriculum

As stated, design, unlike mathematics or physics, does not have a fixed set of standards to follow. Each school has its own conception of the meaning and function of design. For the unsophisticated, these are subtle distinctions and the distinguishing philosophical features of a curriculum which are only appreciated by professionals. Researching educational institutions may only compound the dilemma, for the jargon used in college or art school catalogues only confuses and emphasizes the fact that they are teaching vastly different majors — i.e. visual communications, graphic design, or media arts, to name a few. Programs with comparable fields of concentration in design are not offered by every institution with an art program. There is not uniformity in degrees offered either, so a Bachelor of Fine Arts (B.F.A), Bachelor of Arts (B.A.), or Bachelor of Science (B.S.) may be earned. Moreover, course requirements for the same degree will not necessarily be the same. Compounding the confusion, different programs even receive different accreditation.

Therefore, what distinguishes graphic design programs and how does one become an educated consumer in choosing a school? Furthermore, what is the net result or goal of the educational focus? Perhaps, more directly, what do the best graduate portfolios look like, and is it possible to control what kind of careers the graduates achieve? One excellent way to answer these questions is to ask practicing professionals, especially if they are in a position to evaluate newly graduated and young designers. It is often particularly helpful to know what their own educational and work background has been. They can then possibly be in a position to suggest which schools they might recommend on the basis of their own experience and hiring practices. While their responses will likely be highly subjective, they will nonetheless give a direction.

Faculty: The Key Influence

The curriculum of any art institution is only as strong as the faculty, for in many instances there is no written curriculum but merely a course outline. Therefore, the importance of the faculty input to the overall educational experience and achievement cannot be overemphasized. The teacher's own training and life experience will determine his or her aesthetic value system and may establish different desired levels of professionalism. The classroom situation rests on an ever-changing dynamic between students and instructors. Determining what is good, true and right in art and design is a fundamental, recurring question whose answer is in constant flux.

Part-Time Faculty

It's common practice for most art schools located in a major metropolis to hire instructors who are working professionals for their day-to-day experience and insights. These part-time faculty are individuals that may teach only one class or one day a week. They often teach a specialized subject and bring into the classroom projects from their current work environment. The "real world" atmosphere of these classes simulate, in many respects, a working atelier. Students may be recruited by faculty to work as apprentices in their studios. These experiences can be invaluable and offer a similar value-based level of experiences. Some institutions also actively and aggressively place their students into firms on co-operative work/study programs (co-ops) that offer actual work experience with college credit. The quality of these faculty/student relationships vary in direct correlation to the compatibility of

Work/Study Programs

their personalities. It is very hard to qualify the academic merit, but the pragmatic value becomes self-evident by the quality of the output. In gauging professional art schools, the term "professional" often refers to the number of design or advertising professionals on staff as visiting professors, compared to professional educators. Studying the listing of faculty and their accompanying bios can be more instructional than reading the class syllabus. It is these faculty members, and their point of view formed by their life experience, that will formulate the course content.

Tenured Faculty

Schools may also call upon a sizable pool of professional talent that is not available for long-term teaching commitments, but represents a valuable resource for guest lectures, expert critiques, and intensive workshops. Institutions outside the main city centers use various techniques to fly in critics and guest lecturers, and organize field trips for students, but must rely on a established full-time faculty.

Frequent exposure to the diverse opinions of professionals, as well as their reinforcement of important underlying truths, will better equip the student to make intelligent, necessary career choices. The constant interplay with competent teachers who have specialized in different areas of design can provide desirable role models. The position role models can play in formatting a direction of education should not be undervalued. It is significant. The role model process and the luxury of being exposed to superior talent in a formative period of life are some of the most enriching experiences any education can offer.

In Search of a Contemporary Curriculum

The academic curriculum should also not be overlooked. The graphic designer is an arbiter of the times and must be aware of cultural and political currents. The designer therefore must be have a well-rounded education in order to be sensitive to these issues. It is critical to choose an institution that offers a balanced curriculum. You may also opt for a graduate-level graphic design education which can offer the specialized focus for those who have come from a traditional fine arts/liberal arts education. While this educational direction represents a longer academic degrees the combination of curricula produces an educationally flexible, grounded individual. The more obvious function of post-graduate work is its attraction to graphic designers who have achieved an undergraduate degree in graphic design. The programs most often offer intensified study within a particular design philosophy or simply a return to aesthetic goals after some years of work. While these programs represent a professional enhancement and personal enrichment, they do not represent critical educational requirements in the marketplace.

A Sample of Choices

The American Institute of Graphic Arts publishes a directory of schools offering art programs. The directory includes some 800 institutions. The National Association of Schools for Art and Design in Reston, Virginia lists close to 200 schools in a 80 page directory. The sheer number of choices can be daunting.

The following is a short and highly subjective list of schools, compiled and based on observations during years of reviewing graduating student portfolios. It is a list of only those educational institutions I feel offer significant programs to prepare students to enter the graphic design field. Since the focus of graphic design education is crystallized in the graduates' portfolio, that resulting portfolio has become the hallmark of the educational success of the program as well as the vehicle of entry to that first job. As faculty and program leadership change so do the net effects (the relationship between faculty and syllabus having already been noted), thus this factor must become a consideration to any educational survey.

The wild card in any design education process is always the talent factor, for no matter what the quality of the education is, ultimately talent will out. Just as a mediocre student will not become a major talent no matter how superior the training, a great talent (with sufficient ambition) will overcome major obstacles. Individual creativity is such a strong factor in the finished product (the portfolio) that, ultimately it becomes very clear, that this creativity has the power to surpass any educational dogma. The "individual" quotient in portfolios is also a major factor. Any person in a position to review many portfolios cannot help but observe, just as no two faces or no two fingerprints are alike, neither are two portfolios. For me, that is the mystery and beauty of the process.

How to Contact Colleges

To receive detailed information about a school's programs, admission, tuition, and scholarships contact the admissions office. It is a good idea to ask the admissions office or the placement office about their data on graduates; where the majority find employment. Always check the faculty listings and read their biography. Try to get a sense of the ratio between tenured and visiting faculty. Full-time faculty offer stability and vision to a program; however, sometimes it is the visiting faculty (i.e. working professionals who teach) that give a program its vitality and link to current issues. To get a more personal feel for the program's point of view I would suggest contacting the department chairperson.

It should be noted that New York City, befitting its reputation as The Big Apple, has more graphic design programs than any other major metropolis. The unique quality of these programs existing within the most concentrated work environment and the communications capital of the nation, provides these schools with a large teaching pool of design professionals. It is not unusual for a visiting professor to teach different courses at different schools. Most schools in New York and other metropolitan areas have extensive evening programs as well, which may offer specialized courses, degrees, or programs.

An Educational Short List

The following is an educational short list, divided into three classifications: Undergraduate Graphic Design and Advertising, Undergraduate Industrial Design and Graduate Programs. The institutions with important industrial design programs are indicated by an asterick (*). New York City regional schools are separated because of their unique interrelationship. There is a separate list for graduate programs. These are all institutions which hold significant enough status to be singled out. While these institutions do not guarantee success, they are at the forefront of design education. The bottom line that they student attending a school of repute, who has the innate talent, curiosity, commitment and passion for design and is willing to work hard, will succeed.

Undergraduate Programs

Art Center College of Design*	1700 Lida Street Pasadena, CA 91103 (818) 584-5000
Bringham Young University	Visual Communications Design Provo, UT 84602 (801) 378-3890
California School of Arts and Crafts* (Cal Arts)	1700 17th Street San Francisco, CA 94103 (415) 703-9500

Illinois Institute of Technology

Institute of Design
Chicago, IL 60616
(312) 567-3250

Kansas City Art Institute*

4415 Warwick Boulevard
Kansas City, MO 64111
(816) 561-4852

Kent State University*

School of Art
Kent, OH 44242
(216) 672-2192

Portfolio Center of Atlanta

125 Bennett Street N.W.
Atlanta, GA 30309
(800) 255-3169

Portland School of Art

97 Spring Street
Portland, ME 04101
(207) 775-3052

Rhode Island School of Design*

2 College Street
Providence, RI 02903
(401) 331-3511

Rochester Institute of Technology*

Bauch & Lomb Center
1 Memorial Drive
Rochester, NY 14623

Syracuse University

Department of Visual
Communications
102 Shaffer Art Building
Syracuse, NY 13244
(315) 443-4071

The University of the Arts*

Broad & Pine
Philadelphia, PA 19102
(215) 875-4800

University of Cincinnati*

2624 Clifton Avenue
Cincinnati, OH 45221
(513) 556-6000

New York City region

Cooper Union

41 Cooper Square
New York, NY 10003
(212) 353-4120

Fashion Institute of Technology (FIT)
(State University of New York)

227 West 27th Street
New York, NY 10001-5992
(212) 760-7673

Parsons School of Design

66 Fifth Avenue
New York, NY 10011
(212) 741-8900

Pratt Institute*

School of Art & Design
Brooklyn, NY 11205
(718) 636-3600

School of Visual Arts

209 East 23rd Street
New York, NY 10010-3994
(212) 679-7350

SUNY Purchase
(State University of New York)

735 Anderson Hill Road
Purchase, NY 10577
(914) 251-6000

**Graduate
Programs**

Art Center College of Design, Pasadena, CA

Basel School of Design, Basel, Switzerland

Cranbrook, Bloomfield Hills, MI

Pratt Institute, Brooklyn, NY

Rhode Island School of Design, Providence, RI

Yale, New Haven, CT

Past, Present and Future

15 I n the forward to this book I discussed why everyone should have the luxury of choice. I believe that the importance of recognizing life's choices and following one's intuition is key to realizing individual potential. Sometimes these choices offer surprising opportunities and directions never considered. It's always interesting to ask accomplished people, who seem to have a clear direction to their life, what they thought they were going to be when they began their careers. There are many surprises awaiting in those answers. (Certainly no one grows up saying they want to become a "headhunter"!) In the early stages of a career there is a sense that all the important choices are being made at that time and that the die is permanently cast. Of course, it is a very formative period in one's life, but, having passed through this phase, I can assure you your choices are not complete, and not over. It's no time to rest on past decisions and feel that the hard work is over. As you move into the mature periods of your career, know that the ability to make these transitions is a positive step. What a wonderful way to anticipate the future. It is a future full of choices, full of decisions, full of change — and therefore full of promise.

Change: The Only Constant

It is important to perceive your career as a creative challenge, as one to be molded and formed by many sequential choices. The challenge of a creative career is the ability to achieve continuous progress and advancement. You should always have the sense of growing. The new should be wonderful and exciting, and faced with some apprehension — but not fear. We all know people, and role models, who continue to be vital influences and achievers late into life. And we all know those who seem to be beaten down, tired, and lacking a sense of purpose. Sustaining your intellectual curiosity, energy level, passion and optimism for work and life are critical goals for all to attain. This is how we remain fresh and enjoy the unique gift of creativity.

Fortunately or unfortunately nothing is forever. We all function in a state of flux and things never stay the same. Technology, demographics and economics constantly change the landscape of opportunity. Business, by definition, is in a state of continuous flux. Firms form, grow, and change structure. Perhaps companies downsize or perhaps new partnerships are formed. Clients change, move from company to company, sometimes country to country. Communications styles change, taste levels change — always moving in new directions.

Keeping up is, for most, the hardest chore. And some designers don't keep up. Relying on tried and true formulas, they unhappily learn their proven methods aren't so tried and true. Somehow they have fallen "behind," grown stale — and worse yet, dated. Creative "burnout" is a serious and dangerous problem in design and advertising. We work in a business environment that has an insatiable appetite for the new. The competition is keen (some would say brutal) and the work load very demanding. A continuous new crop of bright young talent entering the scene every year can easily create a justified paranoia for the insecure. This problem becomes an occupational hazard for the person whose talent has not continued onto new plateaus. Unless designers who have lost their spark can move into senior positions with administrative or marketing/sales responsibility, they become the casualties of our creatively driven business, for they can get "tired" without the excitement and enthusiasm of the new.

The Future Belongs to...

Our graphic designer of the future is a fortunate person. This is an individual who will have wonderful resources to draw upon. It is an exciting time. The business is changing.

Graphic Design has felt the same technological, demographic and economic effects over the last ten years as every other segment of our society. The working structure within design firms has changed. The computer is the most obvious addition, along with the amazing demographic swing toward a work force with a female majority. Our designer of the future will function in a world compressed by technology and controlled by economics.

The 1980's witnessed a period of intense merger and acquisition activity. Many advertising agencies and design firms underwent the sometimes painful transitions of unification. Now that partnerships have aged and buy-out agreements have matured, a new structuring and a second generation of leadership is appearing. Some firms, disenchanted with the existing relationships, are buying themselves back. Firms are reconsidering their service offerings. Some are diversifying. Some are reinvestigating the process and methodology of their services. Some see a convergence of design and advertising. Integrated marketing is seen by some as the way to the future. The net effect is that new opportunities are always emerging.

Towards a Global Business Order

A global business order is rapidly evolving. Global marketing is a driving force behind many products and identity programs. The ability to understand foreign languages and customs are increasingly important. New markets in the Pacific rim countries are expanding. After the Japanese commercial explosion, Thailand, Hong Kong, Taiwan, and Korea have become important markets. Vietnam and China will follow. South America is currently perceived by financiers as the next major market for development. The European Eastern Bloc countries are reforming. They will have their own needs and centers for commerce.

The graphic designer will play his or her role all over the

world. Adaptability and flexibility will be important personality traits. The graphic designer of the future will be required
to have the necessary creative talent, to demonstrate the
intellectual savvy for the "big picture," be able to grasp the
marketing strategies, possess the knowledge to access the
latest technology, and exhibit the sensitivity to work with
different cultures. This individual will have to wear many
hats, and assume many guises. The graphic designer will
become a true renaissance personality.

So, always recognize the mark of the future. It is today!

Appendix

Professional Societies. In any discussion of graphic design groups it is helpful to know which professional groups are associated with the area of specialization. These organizations promote their area of interest and offer its membership a variety of enriching programs. The following list represents some of the better-known groups. It may be helpful to contact them for information. Some have membership lists of firms that can be useful when you want to search for a job in another city. They may also be able to give you information about educational programs, seminars, newsletters, annual publications and exhibition programs. These organizations provide the designer the forum to keep up and current as well as an opportunity to network and meet peer groups. The groups marked with an asterisk (*) have regional chapters; always check for those listings locally or with the national organization.

The American Center for Design (ACD)
233 East Ontario, Suite 500
Chicago, IL 60611
(312) 787-2018

The American Institute of Graphic Arts (AIGA)*
(The AIGA has 35 local chapters.)
1059 Third Avenue
New York, NY 10022
(212) 752-0813   (800) 548-1634

The Art Directors Club of New York*
250 Park Avenue South
New York, NY 10003
(212) 674-0550

(There are Art Directors Clubs in many cities, most of whom incorporate the name of the city, such as the ADLA, The Art Directors Club of Los Angeles.)

The Design Management Institute
107 South Street
Boston, MA 02111-2811
(617) 338-6380

The Graphic Artists Guild*
11 West 20 Street, 8th Floor
New York, NY 10011
(212) 463-7730

The Industrial Design Society of America (IDSA)*
1142 Easy Walker Road
Great Falls, VA 22066-1836
(703) 759-0100

The Packaging Designers Council (PDC)*
P.O. Box 1332
Pleasant Valley,
NY 12569
(914) 635-9153

The Society of Environmental Graphic Designers (SEGD) *
47 3rd Street
Cambridge, MA 02141
(617) 577-8225

The Society of Illustrators
128 East 63 Street
New York, NY 10021
(212) 838-2560

The Society of Publication Designers (SPD)
60 East 42nd Street, Suite 1416
New York, NY 10165
(212) 983-8585

Bibliography

AIGA Salary and Benefits Survey, 1992. The American Institute of Graphic Arts, New York, 1992.

American Center for Design. Publications and Video Presentations.

Bayley, Stephen. *Taste.* The Conran Foundation, London, 1983.

Chajet, Clive. *Image By Design From Corporate Vision to Business Reality,* Addison-Wesley, 1991.

Communication Arts. Published eight times a year. Coyne & Blanchard, Palo Alto, CA.

Craig, James. *Graphic Design Career Guide.* Watson-Guptill, New York, 1992.

Crawford, Tad and Eva Doman Bruck. *Business and Legal Forms for Graphic Designers.* Allworth Press, New York. 1990

Crawford, Tad. *Legal Guide for the Visual Artist.* Allworth Press, New York. 1989

Graphic Design: USA. AIGA Annual Book. AIGA, New York.

Graphic Design: USA. Published monthly, Kaye Publishing Corporation, New York.

Graphis. Published bi-monthly, B. Martin Pedersen, New York & Zurich.

Heller, Steven and Lita Talarico. *Design Career.* Van Nostrand Reinhold, New York. 1987.

Heller, Steven. *Graphic Design: New York.* Rockport/Allworth Editions, 1992.

How. Published bi-monthly. F & W Publications, Cincinnati, OH.

Leland, Caryn. *Licensing Art and Design.* Allworth Press, New York. 1990

Lippincott & Margulies. *Identity and Image Management Issues, Chapter 5, No Image, No Premium.* Lippincott & Margulies Inc., New York.

Lippincott & Margulies. *Sense* (a periodical series). Lippincott & Margulies Inc., New York.

National Association of Schools of Art and Design. Directory 92, Reston, VA.

Print. Bi-monthly magazine, RC Publications, Rockville, MD.

Rossol, Monona. *The Artists' Complete Health and Safety Guide.* Allworth Press, New York. 1990

Sebastian, Liane. *Electronic Design and Publishing: Business Practices.* Allworth Press, New York, 1992

Step-By-Step Graphics. Published monthly, SBS Publishing, Peoria, IL.

The Art Directors Club Annual. A book published annually by The Art Directors Club of New York.

The Design Management Institute. *The Design Management Journal* (quarterly series). The Design Management Press, Boston, MA.

The Joint Ethics Committee, Code of Fair Practice, The Joint Ethics Committee, New York, 1989.

SEGD Messages. Published quarterly, The Society of Environmental Graphic Designers, Cambridge, MA.

Typography. The Annual of the Type Directors Club, New York.

Index

About the Author

Roz Goldfarb is the founder and president of Roz Goldfarb Associates, Inc. (RGA), a New York-based recruitment firm specializing in design, advertising and marketing personnel. The firm's clients are the leaders in every category of the global marketing communications and business worlds.

Ms. Goldfarb formed RGA in 1985. The new firm, focused on "civilized headhunting" and career management, quickly grew to include an impressive national and international client roster. Today, Roz Goldfarb Associates' reputation is as the premier company for search and recruitment.

Before entering the recruitment field, Ms. Goldfarb concentrated her energies in the field of higher education, where career issues became one of her main concerns. From 1970–1979 she was a member of the administration and faculty of Pratt Institute, and from 1974–1979 she was the Director of the Pratt Phoenix School of Design. While at Pratt she wrote the curriculum for Pratt's Associate Degree Program. Other work for Pratt included the development of seminars, workshops and lecture series, as well as international programs in France and Denmark. It was these experiences as an educator, coupled with her activities as a recruiter, that brought her to the attention of the Parsons School of Design. From 1980–1986, she was a consultant to Parsons for the development of their Professional Placement Office. She currently holds the position of Chairperson with Pratt Institute's National Alumni Council.

Highly committed to the design field, Ms. Goldfarb established a scholarship in the name of her firm, in 1987, to further the education of talented college-level design students who require scholarship aid. The scholarship is administered through the Art Directors Club of New York.

Ms. Goldfarb frequently addresses professional groups. These groups have included The Aspen International Design Conference, the Art Directors Clubs of New York and Los Angeles, the New York and Cleveland chapters of The American Institute of Graphic Arts, the On the Edge seminar at the Grand Canyon, and the Art Directors and Artists Club of Sacramento. She has also spoken to student groups on career opportunities and the changing design environment at the Art Center College of Design, Pratt Institute, the Parsons School of Design, the School of Visual Arts, Kent State and Syracuse University.

Ms. Goldfarb holds a Master of Fine Arts degree in sculpture from Pratt Institute and a Bachelor of Arts degree from Hunter College of the City of New York, where she studied painting with Robert Motherwell.

A native New Yorker, Ms. Goldfarb is married, has three daughters and one grandson. She is passionate about 13th and 14th century Italian Art and the opera, and collects Southwest Indian pottery and jewelry, ancient glass and modern abstract prints.

Allworth Books

Allworth Press publishes quality books to help individuals and small businesses. Titles include:

Legal-Wise: Self-Help Legal Forms for Everyone *by Carl W. Battle* (208 pages, 8½" X 11", $16.95)

Senior Counsel: Legal and Financial Strategies for Age 50 and Beyond *by Carl W. Battle* (256 pages, 6¾" X 10", $16.95)

Business and Legal Forms for Authors and Self-Publishers *by Tad Crawford* (176 pages, 8⅞" X 11", $15.95)

Business and Legal Forms for Fine Artists *by Tad Crawford* (128 pages, 8⅞" X 11", $12.95)

Business and Legal Forms for Graphic Designers *by Tad Crawford and Eva Doman Bruck* (208 pages, 8½" X 11", $19.95)

Business and Legal Forms for Illustrators *by Tad Crawford* (160 pages, 8⅞" X 11", $15.95)

Business and Legal Forms for Photographers *by Tad Crawford* (192 pages, 8½" X 11", $18.95)

Legal Guide for the Visual Artist *by Tad Crawford* (224 pages, 7" X 12", $18.95)

How to Sell Your Photographs and Illustrations *by Elliott and Barbara Gordon* (128 pages, 8" X 10", $16.95)

The Business of Being an Artist *by Dan Grant* (224 pages, 6" X 9", $16.95)

On Becoming an Artist *by Dan Grant* (192 pages, 6" X 9", $12.95)

The Family Legal Companion *by Thomas Hauser* (256 pages, 6" X 9", $16.95)

How to Shoot Stock Photos that Sell *by Michal Heron* (192 pages, 8" X 10", $16.95)

The Photographer's Organizer *by Michal Heron* (192 pages, 28" X 10", $16.95)

Stock Photo Forms *by Michal Heron* (32 pages, 8½" X 11", $8.95)

Accepted: Your Guide to Finding the Right College —and How to Pay for It *by Stuart Kahan* (128 pages, 6¾" X 10", $10.95)

The Photographer's Assistant *by John Kieffer* (208 pages, 6¾" X 10", $16.95)

Licensing Art & Design *by Caryn R. Leland* (272 pages, 6" X 9", $18 .95)

Travel Photography: A Complete Guide to How to Shoot and Sell *by Susan McCartney* (384 pages, 6¾" X 10", $22.95)

The Graphic Designer's Basic Guide to the MacIntosh *by Michael Meyerowitz and Sam Sanchez* (144 pages, 8" X 10", $19.95)

Hers: The Wise Woman's Guide to Starting a Business on $2,000 or Less *by Carol Milano* (208 pages, 6" X 9", $12.95)

The Artist's Complete Health and Safety Guide *by Monona Rossol* (328 pages, 6" X 9", $16.95)

Stage Fright *by Monona Rossol* (144 pages, 6" X 9", $12.95)

The Unemployment Survival Handbook *by Nina Schuyler* (144 pages, 6" X 9", $9.95)

Electronic Design and Publishing: Business Practices *by Liane Sebastian* (112 pages, 6¾" X 10", $19.95)

Overexposure: Health Hazards in Photography *by Susan Shaw and Monona Rossol* (320 pages, 6¾" X 10", $18.95)

Caring for Your Art *by Jill Snyder* (176 pages, 6" X 9", $14.95)

Make It Legal *by Lee Wilson* (272 pages, 6" X 9", $18 .95)

Please write to request our free catalog. If you wish to order a book, send your check or money order to:
Allworth Press, 10 East 23rd Street, Suite 400, New York, New York 10010
To pay for shipping and handling, include $3 for the first book ordered and $1 for each additional book ($7 plus $1 if the order is from Canada). New York State residents must add sales tax.